The Old House Book

The Old House Book

Robin Langley Sommer

PROSPERO
B·O·O·K·S
A DIVISION OF CHAPTERS INC.

Page 1 photograph:
A decorative pediment centered on a pineapple, a traditional sign of welcome.

Page 2 photograph:
Colonial townhouses in Philadelphia's historic Elfreth's Alley.

Page 4 photographs:
Appliqué and carving on façades from (l. to r.) San Francisco, Philadelphia and Portland, Maine.

Page 5 photographs:
Ornamental metalwork door details from (l. to r.) Philadelphia, Newport and Charleston.

Published by Saraband Inc., PO Box 0032, Rowayton, CT 06853-0032, USA

This edition produced for Prospero Books, a division of Chapters, Inc.

Copyright © 1999 Saraband Inc.

Design © Ziga Design

ISBN: 1-55267-967-5

Printed in China

10 9 8 7 6 5 4 3 2 1

FOR BETH, WITH LOVE AND GRATITUDE

Contents

Introduction

The rich and diverse legacy of North American architecture is being reclaimed wholeheartedly by contemporary Americans and Canadians who seek the presence of the past in their homes and communities. In the postmodern age, this is more than an exercise in nostalgia. The restlessness and rootlessness of popular culture have created a deep need for reconnection with the shared values, beliefs and sense of solidarity without which the human community ceases to function as such and eventually falls apart.

The growing tendency to seek out the best of the past and adapt it to the present is reflected in our interest in old houses, churches, public buildings, barns and other artefacts that foster a sense of continuity in both the manmade and natural environments. We see it in the expansion of efforts to conserve open land, endangered animals, major landmarks. It is also apparent in the renewed interest in craftsmanship and other creative endeavors that sustained our predecessors in an ever-changing world. They may have faced more physical dangers and hardships than we do today, but they shared a sense of community that is far less prevalent in our hard-driving, high-tech society.

This pictorial history of North American dwelling styles prior to the modern era traces the ethnic and cultural roots of our residential

Opposite: *A New England cottage in Belfast, Maine, with a flower-bordered brick path.*

Left: *Thatched-roof cottages of the kind built by the Pilgrims in the early 1600s are recreated at Plimouth Plantation in Plymouth, Massachusetts.*

Above: *A rambling Amish family farmstead established by nineteenth-century pioneers, who left Pennsylvania for Holmes County, Ohio.*

architecture from the earliest colonial structures to the turn of the twentieth century. It explores the many variations of the post-medieval English cottage, the Scandinavian and Middle European log cabin, the Spanish colonial adobe house, the French Creole dwellings that became widespread in what was long known as the New World. The Cape Cod-style house that we see today is recognizable as a direct descendant of the cottages built on the shifting sands of the Massachusetts coastline by early English settlers. The substantial Dutch colonial style retained its influence in the Hudson Valley and the mid-Atlantic region long after the influence of the Dutch East India Company was eclipsed by British conquest.

Similarly, the Acadian dwellings of French settlers in southwestern Quebec and the future Atlantic Provinces of Canada were transplanted to the lower Mississippi Valley and adapted to the demands of a hot, humid climate thousands of miles from their place of origin. It is a fascinating story, replete with imaginative solutions to new challenges posed by major shifts in pop-

ulation, culture and historical perspective. It is also a personal history, written in wood, brick, stone, sod, glass and metal by men and women who struck roots in alien soil and made it their own by shaping the built and natural landscapes to meet their needs.

The growing prosperity of the original European settlers soon manifested itself in larger, more comfortable dwellings designed to accommodate growing families and to show their builders' affluence and good taste. Pattern books imported from England guided domestic carpenters and building tradesmen in the proportions of the fashionable eighteenth-century Georgian style. Soon, domestic pattern books became available, acknowledging their debt to British architecture but striking out in new directions, as seen in the Federal and Jeffersonian Classical styles. They asserted the autonomy of the newly created United States after the Revolutionary War. In British Columbia, on the other hand, the Georgian style remained paramount long after 1783, evolving into the closely related Adam and Regency styles of the early nineteenth century.

Below: *Crude frame and sod shelters built in the Arctic for the summer months are dwarfed by the vast land- and seascapes of this remote region.*

However, the many variations on Georgian architecture in both countries retained their affinity with the tenets of classical design. Its influence is shown in the fact that Georgian houses generally comprise three zones: a short base—the visual foundation—a longer central zone with symmetrical elements, and a shorter top story that reprises the restrained decorative embellishments of the other levels.

The abundance of timber in North America dictated that many house designs would be executed in wood by skilled carpenters, even those

Right: *Montreal's Sheriff Gray House (1876) is typical of Quebec provincial architecture, with fieldstone walls overlaid with plaster and casement windows in simple surrounds.*

based on masonry models. Fieldstone, also called rubblestone, and brick made from local clay, were used for vernacular housing, while expensive dwellings and public buildings were often constructed of cut stone, including granite, marble, limestone and sandstone, quarried first in New England and Quebec and later, farther west.

Some regions retained their traditional styles for centuries, and their influence is apparent today long after most of the original buildings have succumbed to the elements, disuse, or shifting centers of population. In Nova Scotia, for example, the original vernacular house style is readily discernible in two-story frame construction with a central gable on a three-bay façade. The familiar nineteenth-century New York City brownstone (actually sandstone) shares traits with the London townhouse of an earlier day, and the typical Southwestern adobe dwelling has altered little in its basic plan for several hundred years, although new construction materials and methods have come into use.

Among the styles described and illustrated here, at least a dozen will be familiar to the average reader, who may be more of an authority on architecture than he or she knows. Hopefully, the old houses pictured throughout this book will make it easier to identify simi-

lar buildings in one's own community, region and travel destinations.

As we will see, early colonial houses on the East Coast were based largely on medieval prototypes, which had asymmetrical façades and small casement windows. During the eighteenth century, there was a movement toward classical balance, with larger casement windows more evenly spaced around a central entryway. England's Georgian style, seen first in Boston and eastern Canada, became increasingly influential. It was reflected in house plans balanced around a central axis, with minimal decoration. Sash windows with rectangular panes largely replaced the casement window. Other hallmarks of the style include a modest doorway flanked by pilasters and crowned by a simple pediment, and a hipped roof with paired chimneys at either end.

German colonial houses were often constructed of stone over heavy timber framing. They had thick walls, slightly arched doorways and windows and an attic story with several dormers. Dutch colonial buildings often combined wood with brick or stone under an overhanging roof. Settlers from Sweden and Germany built log cabins of various styles that eventually became identified with frontier life in both the United States and Canada. Timber was becoming scarce in Europe when the early colonists arrived, but the New World was so heavily forested that the supply of wood seemed, at first, to be inexhaustible.

After the American Revolution, the classical Federal style evolved away from Georgian models toward more flexible, less formal plans. Archaeological findings at Pompeii and Herculaneum, Italy, influenced this style, which often incorporates rotundas and other features of Roman architecture, as seen in Thomas Jefferson's Monticello, Virginia. It was especially inflential in the South, where the new national capital at Washington, D.C., set the tone for the region. Later, Regency and Adam-style details were incorporated as ornaments, including urns, garlands, swags and the characteristic semicircular fanlight over the main entrance.

The popular Greek Revival style of the early 1800s is seen in both houses and public buildings. It emphasized severe rectilinear proportions and the use of columns or pilasters, often several stories high. The moderately sloped roofline incorporated pediments, moldings and sometimes Roman forms—rounded arches and domes. Even simple wooden cottages acquired modest pediments and columnar porch supports, as this "democratic" style became prevalent nationwide.

After about 1830, the contrasting Gothic Revival movement reflected the growing interest in the picturesque, which spread rapidly under the influence of A.J. Downing, whose books, including *The Architecture of Country Houses*, popularized the style. It is recognized by asymmetrical façades; vertical elements including towers, finials and pointed arches; and the use of carved and pierced woodwork along the eaves, produced by special machine saws that imitated expensive stone tracery. Steeply gabled roofs carried out the vertical theme, and bay windows and oriels (upper-story bays) often incorporated stained glass.

Porches first became a feature on early American houses in the South, and eventually, their use spread across the continent, on everything from miners' shacks and shanties to ele-

gant suburban mansions. The porch (or piazza, in its refined incarnation) offered sheltered living space outdoors, relief from summer heat and a place for families and friends to gather and share news of the day. It increased the sense of community, even in working-class urban rowhouses, where the "front stoop" brought neighbors together.

As the United States and Canada grew in population and prosperity, familiar vernacular styles were altered or replaced by the rapidly changing fashions of the Victorian age. Eclecticism was the hallmark of the period, ranging from the fashionable Italianate and French Empire styles to the exuberant Queen Anne, which used a multitude of colors, textures and forms to create a distinctive look. In its townhouse form, the Queen Anne is seen in San Francisco's famous "painted ladies," and countless suburban examples have also been

Below: *This modest Colonial townhouse in Philadelphia was the home of Betsy Ross, credited with the design of the original "star-spangled banner."*

Above: *Elegant Davenport House, in Savannah, Georgia, is a study in restrained classicism.*

Opposite: *The Gothic Revival John B. McCreary House ("the Abbey") in Cape May, New Jersey (1869–70).*

a coherent style by the use of shingle cladding. The fashion spread rapidly from the East Coast to the Midwest, where it was adopted by many up-and-coming young architects, including Frank Lloyd Wright in the earliest phase of his career. The Shingle-style house he built for his own family in suburban Oak Park, Illinois, caused some of his neighbors to comment disparagingly, "Seaside," but this home-studio would become one of the nation's best-known buildings, as a testing ground for the ideas of a towering figure in twentieth-century architecture and design.

In its more formal aspect, Richardson's style embraced the massive masonry forms of the Romanesque Revival: rounded arches, thick columns and towers with conical caps, deeply recessed windows and doorways, polychrome or patterned masonry. Richardsonian Romanesque is seen primarily in such outstanding public buildings as Boston's Trinity Church, as well as in the impressive stone mansions designed for several wealthy East Coast and Midwestern clients.

The last great wave of nineteenth-century architecture was the Renaissance Revival or Beaux-Arts style, so called because its practitioners had studied at the prestigious *École des Beaux Arts* in Paris (at this time, the Massachusetts Institute of Technology had the first and one of the only schools of architecture in the United States). Beaux-Arts architects drew upon three centuries of Renaissance detail, especially as seen in French architecture, to produce imposing mansions and public buildings, including those in the Chateauesque mode, like North Carolina's vast Biltmore estate and the great railroad hotels and resorts from Quebec to Alberta, Canada.

lovingly restored by a new generation of owners. While the stark International style was at its height, realtors shunned the very word "Victorian," but in recent years it has become a major inducement to prospective buyers.

Several styles indigenous to the United States emerged during the late 1800s, influenced by a series of gifted young architects, including the highly creative Henry Hobson Richardson (1838-86). His informal Shingle style was widely adopted for large resort homes in which the varying elements were united into

In all its manifestations, our built landscape has much to tell us about ourselves and our cultural history. It forms a bridge between past and present, allowing us to select from both spheres those elements that are most meaningful to us today and important for tomorrow, not merely in terms of shelter, but in the larger realm of communal images, ideas and aspirations.

Colonial Styles, Town and Country

T ime and again, the original colonial styles of North American architecture have been reprised, adapted and embellished for new generations. Their unique suitability to the various regions where they first sheltered immigrants from the Old World gave both character and continuity to emergent communities along the Atlantic seaboard, from Quebec to St. Augustine, Florida. Ethnic roots in seventeenth-century France, England, Spain, Germany, the Netherlands and Scandinavia flowered into distinctive new forms on North American soil, and although few of the original colonial buildings have survived, they have left their imprint on the houses we live in today.

The English cottage was transplanted to New England in 1620 with the Pilgrim settlers who landed in Plymouth, Massachusetts. Based on medieval Elizabethan models, early American shelters consisted of thick post-and-beam frames rising to steep gabled roofs covered by thatch. Thin wall studs were insulated with woven twigs (wattle) covered with mud or clay, called daub. The building was then sheathed with hand-split clapboards for weatherproofing. Windows were very small because of the cold climate, and were covered in winter with oiled paper in the absence of glass.

Most of these dwellings consisted of a single large room with a storage loft above. They were heated by fieldstone fireplaces with wattle-and-daub chimneys, and the flammable thatched roofs—made of sewn grass or tufts of reed—often resulted in house fires. These cramped, smoky shelters were a far cry from the English cottage

Opposite: *A well-preserved masonry building in the German style, once a custom house on the Potomac Canal near Washington, D.C.*

Left: *The historic Thomas Ash House, a New England colonial built in 1790 at Stonington, Connecticut. The shutters were probably a later addition.*

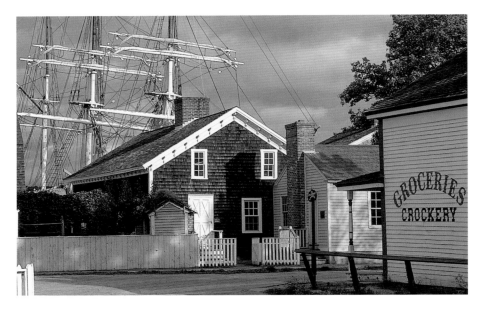

Above: *Mystic Seaport, Connecticut, exemplifies the vernacular style of a coastal whaling town, with its shingled houses and clapboard shops.*

we visualize today, with cozy sun-filled rooms and casement windows overlooking flower boxes and an informal garden filled with old-fashioned plants in splendid disarray. All this would have seemed like a dream to the Pilgrims of Plymouth and Salem, who surrounded their first homes with wooden palisades to keep out wild animals and potentially hostile natives.

Farther south, English colonists had struggled to establish themselves in Virginia since 1585. But it was not until forty years later that the Jamestown colony, within its triangular palisade on the James River, began to flourish. Its post-and-beam houses were similar to those of New England, but the milder climate allowed much of the framing to be left exposed, with wattle-and-daub infill between the diagonally braced posts. (Known as half-timbering, this style is familiar to us through the Tudor Revival houses dating from the nineteenth century, although their exposed timbers served a purely decorative rather than a structural function.) The fireplace and its chimney protruded from an end wall, reducing heat inside when cooking, especially during the summer.

Another modified cottage style was the "stone ender," built by English settlers of Rhode Island from about 1645. It was named for the massive stone fireplace with medieval-style chimney that took up most of an end wall. Amenities including small leaded casement windows with diamond-shaped panes were imported from England, and by 1690 the bedroom area under

the eaves might have dormers to allow for more light and space upstairs.

When a lean-to shed was built onto the back as a kitchen area, the house resembled a medieval saltbox in shape, and this indigenous style became popular from Atlantic Canada to southern Connecticut. As families prospered, they expanded the saltbox to include a full second story, or an extra bedroom and pantry on either side of the kitchen. The kitchen addition shared the ground-floor fireplace and had its own flue, comprising a second chimney beside the first. The long slope of the north-facing roof provided protection from winter winds and shed snow and rain. This versatile style resulted in many local variations, including the Nantucket Island whaler's house, with a lean-to shed on both sides of a gable end, and the L-shaped "outshot" house, which, like Topsy, "just grew" as a cluster of lean-tos was added over the years.

Contemporaneous with the saltbox was the two-story garrison house of southern New England, in which the second story overhung the first in medieval fashion. Built from about 1670, these houses were covered with split-cedar clapboards nailed to an oak frame (cedar was widely used for siding and roofing because of its durability). The garrison house had a steep gable roof with large centered chimneys. Some were ornamented with hand-carved acorn-shaped pendants below the overhang—usually two on either side of the centered front entrance. Garrison-house prototypes included the gabled townhouses that had emerged in crowded London during the late 1500s and the two-story blockhouses of early colonial forts.

The log cabin so closely identified with frontier life originated with Swedish settlers to the Delaware Valley from about 1638. Later, German immigrants brought their own log-building techniques, called *Fachwerk*, to this region from south-central Europe—framing made of heavy timbers. Three basic log-cabin forms emerged over a 200-year period and spread from the Delaware and Ohio River Valleys to the trans-Mississippi plains, where sod replaced scarce timber as the basic building material.

The original log cabin was a single-room structure in which the log walls were joined at the corners by various types of notching. Split-log rafters covered with cedar shingles formed the roof. In most cases, the bark was removed before construction to prevent decay. A stone fireplace protruded from one end of the cabin, and the chimney was built of mud-lined sticks. Later developments included the two-room "saddlebag" cabin (1740) and the "dogtrot" cabin (1840), which are discussed in chapters 2 and 3.

By 1690 the New England farmhouse had a recognizable form that marked the transition from rough-and-ready colonial housing to the more refined Georgian style imported from England. These rectangular dwellings ranged from one-and-one-half to two-and-one-half stories (the latter was called the New England Large). They had massive central chimneys serving several fireplaces and double-hung sash windows arranged symmetrically around a central entryway. From about 1740, craftsmen newly arrived from England began to add decorative details, including paneled doors flanked by pilasters and crowned by carved pediments. Skilled builders and carpenters armed with pattern books soon mastered the style.

Like their predecessors, Georgian houses were of braced oak-frame construction covered with clapboards, but wooden flooring and interior walls of plaster over strips of wooden lathing made them more comfortable and attractive. They would be constructed widely for more than a hundred years, and their restrained classical symmetry is still a strong influence on residential architecture, especially along the Atlantic coast.

After the Revolutionary War, the newly independent United States turned away from Georgian models to the Federal style, including Jeffersonian Classicism, while eastern Canada's original French colonial style was augmented by British incursions. When the British captured Quebec in 1759, they retained the sensible building codes of the French government, which reduced the risk of fire by encouraging the use of fieldstone building materials in urban centers. Atlantic Canada employed both masonry and woodworking techniques brought by settlers from the British Isles and New England. In Nova Scotia, the English-speaking population doubled in 1783 with the immigration of Loyalists and Quakers from the original thirteen colonies who rejected the American Revolution for political and religious reasons.

The earliest permanent buildings in New France were those of Quebec, based on the late medieval style of northern France. They consisted of squared timbers set upright on a sill and infilled with fieldstone, or a mixture of mud and stone. By the mid-seventeenth century, this method was being replaced by all-wood construction of the kind called *piéces-sur-piéces*, or piece-on-piece. Short squared timbers were slotted into place between the uprights to form walls, then covered with horizontal planks. Mud was often used as insulation between the walls to keep the wind and cold out. Openings were few and evenly spaced, and lighter timber roof frames resulted in the characteristic bellcast roof flare of Quebec architecture.

Below: *A frame house typical of Atlantic Canada, in Hart's Cove, Newfoundland.*

Right: *The pre-Revolutionary Davis Lenox House (1759), in Philadelphia, is an excellent example of the colonial townhouse.*

At first, all-masonry construction in New France was reserved for public buildings, including churches and seminaries. Where native stone was employed, it was usually plastered over and crowned by a mansard roof. Classical details imported from France included pediments, corner quoins (stone blocks inset to form a pattern) and carved moldings. The Quebec townhouse, seen also in Old Montreal, took on a distinctive form in the eighteenth century. Up to four stories high, it was built of fieldstone, with multipaned casement windows trimmed in smooth stone. High end walls on the steeply sloping gable roof served as fire breaks. The rural *maison traditionelle* was a long structure of wood or stone with a hipped roof, flared at the eaves, and dormers to light the top story. French colonial style would become influential in the Mississippi Valley, as seen in chapters 2 and 3.

Although Dutch hegemony in the New World ended in 1664 with British conquest, the Dutch colonial style made itself felt far longer. Concentrated in New York's Hudson Valley, New Jersey, Long Island and New Amsterdam (New York City), Dutch farmers built sturdy one-and-one-half-story houses of stone and timber with brick veneering, and long house-barns like those of the Netherlands. Dutch townhouses in New Amsterdam, Albany and Kingston (originally Wittwyck), New York, were one or two stories tall and several rooms deep, with front gables facing the street. Brick veneering was applied to the façade in accordance with the fire laws, but the wooden cladding on the other three sides was often exposed.

Many of the early Dutch townhouses had stepped or curvilinear Flemish gables. The two-sloped gambrel roof, which is usually considered Dutch in origin, was, in fact, probably imported by English builders in the mid-eighteenth century. The oldest collection of Dutch colonial houses on the continent has been preserved at the Richmondtown Restoration on New York's Staten Island.

Spanish architectural influence began in 1565, with the founding of St. Augustine, Florida, an outpost to protect the mother country's sailing ships. Its first shelters, built within walled compounds, were one-room palmetto-frond huts modeled on those of the native Seminole. Soon, simple board houses similar to the huts came into use. They had walls and gables of wide board siding nailed to wooden frames, and retained thatched roofs with smoke holes rather than chimneys. A century later, the colonial city of Pensacola was established on the Gulf Coast. Over time, Spanish Florida extended its influence as far north as present-day South Carolina, and indigenous building materials were developed. They included tabby—a cementlike mix of oyster shells, lime and sand—and coquina stone, sedimentary rock formed by dense layers of coquina shells.

By the eighteenth century, larger houses were formed by adding rooms in line, centered around a Spanish patio. In this hot climate, kitchens were detached from the main house, loggias took advantage of breezes and balconied second stories were supported on projecting wooden joists (*vigas*), as seen also in the Hispanic Southwest. The Southeastern Spanish style was influenced by settlers from the Canary Islands and the Caribbean, while that of the Southwest drew heavily upon indigenous Pueblo styles and materials, including adobe, which had also been used in Spain's vernacular architecture.

From about 1540 through the Mexican period, ending in the late 1840s with U.S. conquest from New Mexico to Northern California, Southwestern architecture became identified with flat roofs supported on timber *vigas*, roofing of curved red-clay tile, Roman arches, hooded and bell-shaped fireplaces, and single-room-deep plans enclosing a patio. As Joe S. Graham observes in *America's Architectural Roots* (National Trust for Historic Preservation, 1986): "Spanish colonial architecture has left a profound imprint on the cultural landscape of the Southwest. It has been the basis for the major regional styles, including the Monterey style of California and the Spanish Colonial style found in California and Texas. One of the most distinctive is the Santa Fe (also called Spanish-Pueblo) style of New Mexico."

From about 1675, German immigrants to the Delaware Valley built small farmhouses with fieldstone walls or exposed framing of heavy timber, called *Fachwerk*. Entered through the kitchen, they had a *stuba*, or common room, that shared the central kitchen fireplace. As in the Rhineland, gabled roofs were supported by complex framing. As prosperity increased, German settlers expanded into a second story and began to ornament their houses with rich interior woodwork and painting. The original half-timbered style was often adapted to a fieldstone ground floor with a second floor of notched log. The gable roof had a massive stone chimney.

By the early eighteenth century, the style that would become known (confusingly enough) as "Pennsylvania Dutch" was common in eastern Pennsylvania and reached as far north as eastern Canada. (The misnomer resulted from corruption of the German word *Deutsch*, meaning German, to Dutch.) These substantial stone houses and their barns were often built partly into a hillside (banked) to provide winter insulation and summer cooling. Two-story masonry "country townhouses" also became popular in urban areas, especially Philadelphia, and in rural Maryland, Virginia and North Carolina.

From about 1800, many German dwellings gained a one-and-one-half-story kitchen addition and short, sloping pent roofs over entrances, to keep off rain and snow. Wooden paneling inside offset the winter cold and dampness inherent in stone construction. Throughout this period, the influence of settlers from Sweden, Finland, Switzerland and the British Isles also made itself felt in regional borrowings and adaptations throughout the Delaware Valley area.

Left: *Davenport House in Savannah, Georgia, built in the early 1800s, is a handsome example of the late-Georgian Adam style in its classical symmetry and detailing.*

The Spirit of New England

Gabled roofs with central chimneys, shingle cladding,
symmetrical façades and double-hung sash windows
distinguish these colonial cottages in Maine. The upper
stories, lit only by windows on the gable ends, would have
been used originally as storage attics. The house above, in
Pemaquid Falls, shows the simple lines and clean proportions
of this classic style. On the opposite page: the Swift-Daily
House (top), maintained by the Easton Historical Museum;
and Chapman Hall (below), built in Newcastle in 1754.

In Wood and Stone

The sturdy German colonial stone house on the opposite page was built in 1804 in Kutztown, Pennsylvania. Note the many small panes of the sash windows in their simple white frames. At right is a Federal-style house with Greek Revival detailing (1850) in the historic district of New Albany, Indiana. Below is a faithful replica of the medieval-English Cotswold stone cottage, in which the roofline slopes to ground level on one side (Greenfield Village, Michigan).

Eighteenth-century Gambrel Roofs

All three of these New England houses have the two-sloped gambrel roof introduced to the original thirteen colonies by English builders and widely associated with the Dutch colonial styles. The Dwight House, below, built about 1725 in Springfield, Massachusetts, has been relocated to the historic village of Deerfield and restored as a museum. On the opposite page are the Reverend Thomas Hawley House (right) in Ridgefield, Connecticut (1714–15), and (below) the Dutch colonial Nathan Hale House in Coventry, Connecticut, bounded by the fieldstone wall characteristic of the region, where the soil had to be cleared of many stones before planting.

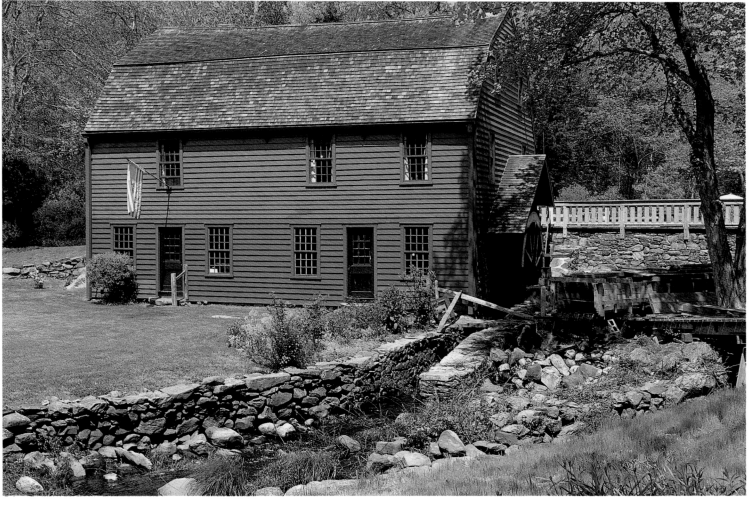

Spanish Colonial Influence

The nineteenth-century LaBorde House (above), in Rio Grande City, Texas, shows the Hispanic style that originated in colonial Mexico in its central two-story colonnade, which is detailed in the Victorian mode. At left is the Elms' Court Carriage House in Natchez, Mississippi, with parapeted gables and deep window embrasures reminiscent of Spanish forts and churches.

Archways and Courtyards

Epitomizing the Southwestern colonial style is the Spanish Governor's Palace (1749) in San Antonio, Texas. The stone fountain in the courtyard is a familiar feature; so is the arched entryway in the adobe wall and the *vigas* (timber roof supports) protruding from the façade.

Medieval Antecedents

These New England houses show their Elizabethan heritage in their roof and chimney styles, overhanging eaves and weatherclad timber framing. The oldest example is the Samuel Pickman House (opposite, top), built about 1681 in Salem, Massachusetts, which was founded by the Pilgrims. Below it is the Ebenezer Beeman House (1745), called Clover Nook, in Warren, Connecticut. The Ridgefield, Connecticut, farmhouse below dates from 1750, but has been modified by the addition of an entry porch and new windows.

The Saltbox Style

Classic examples of the indigenous saltbox house, with its
long-sloped north-facing roof, dot the Atlantic coastline. The
one above is the oldest house on Nantucket Island,
Massachusetts, a whaling community founded in the early
1700s. Later houses in this style (opposite) were photographed
in Kent (above) and Ridgefield, Connecticut. Massive central
chimneys and lean-to additions are characteristic of saltbox
houses, which were transplanted to the West Coast by
homesick New Englanders during the nineteenth century.

By Way of England

The classic early Georgian house above, in scenic
Stockbridge, Massachusetts, dates from 1739. Its only
decoration is the scrolled pediment and carved pilasters
at the entry. Window glazing features nine panes in the upper
sash and six in the lower. On the opposite page (above) is
a New England Large colonial farmhouse in Wiscasset,
Maine, with an atypical single dormer at the attic level.
Below it, the shingled Georgian Winslow Crocker House
in Yarmouthport, Massachusetts, has modest window
surrounds painted white and a transom of six panes above
the decorative doorway.

Maritime Charm

The rectangular, red-roofed seaside cottage opposite, beautiful in its simplicity, lies on the exposed rocky coast of Fogo Island, Newfoundland. This dwelling is typical of those built by British settlers—mainly fishermen and farmers—in the Maritime Provinces. An abandoned farmhouse with shed-roofed dormer on Prince Edward Island (right) succumbs to the elements, its timber framework buckling under the assaults of wind and weather. Below is a well-kept working farm on the island, with a steeply gabled houseroof to shed snow and a gambrel-roofed barn.

French Town Houses

Seventeenth-century Montreal, Quebec, lives on in its cobblestoned Old City. At left is a wooden house with fieldstone chimney and foundation on Rue Saint-Louis—the only surviving faubourg home (outside the original fortifications) in Montreal. Below is the Beaudouin House, with rough-cut plastered fieldstone walls, built for a city official in 1786.

Enduring Fieldstone

Above is the Chateau Ramezay (1705) in Montreal, a large
maison de ville that has served as a governor's mansion,
military headquarters, courthouse and museum. The Pierre
du Calvet House (right), built by a Huguenot merchant,
shows the S-shaped iron bars that helped support the
structure, and the high end walls that were mandated
as firebreaks after a disastrous city fire in 1721.

Georgian Classics

Salem, Massachusetts, merchant Elias Derby built the house
above, overlooking Derby Wharf, in 1762 to keep a close eye
on his shipping enterprises. Note the dentils (tooth-shaped
ornamentation) along the cornice line and in the pediment
above the doorway. Protruding brick bands, called stringcourses, mark the foundation line and the second-story level.
On the opposite page, the Van Ness House (above), built in
Red Hook, New York, in 1797 shows more elaborate
detailing, as seen in the portico with Palladian window above,
which reflects the neoclassical Federal style. Below it is a later
post-Revolutionary house in Portland, Maine, which retains
the symmetrical elements of late Georgian architecture
despite its large size and diverse window treatments.

Federal and Georgian Styles

At left is the Wright House (1824) in Deerfield, Massachusetts, a brick house in the Federal style now serving as a museum of Chinese porcelain and early American furniture. Below, the elegant Hunter House (1748) in Newport, Rhode Island, has a rooftop balustrade known as a "widow's walk" in coastal New England—a vantage point from which captains' wives could watch hopefully for the safe return of incoming ships.

Town and Country

Below, another historic Newport house— clapboard on a raised foundation—with a graceful entry flanked by a double stairway. At right, a New England brick farmhouse in Chester, Vermont, with an elliptical arch over the central doorway, which has shutters for its sidelights. As in the South, shutters were often installed in northern New England to protect the windows from heavy storms and high winds.

The Southern Styles

The phrase "Southern style" usually calls up images of spacious, elegant prebellum plantation houses, but these mansions are only one facet of a diverse regional architecture that began with the English cottages at Jamestown and included the Regency-style townhouses of post-Civil War Savannah, Georgia.

As early as 1635, English settlers in the Chesapeake region, on the mid-Atlantic coast, were building relatively substantial houses of timber framing and brick, made from tidewater clay, which gave rise to the term "Tidewater house." Maryland's original one-room cottages with lofts, based on the "hall," or nuclear building unit of medieval England, soon expanded into the hall-and-parlor house with the addition of a ground-floor kitchen (the parlor) and several dormers in the sleeping loft to increase light and space. Access to these lofts was by steep wooden stairs in a corner of the main room. Twin brick chimneys at the gable ends marked the addition of a kitchen fireplace to the original single-chimney dwelling.

Before 1700 colonists in Virginia and Maryland were digging cellars in which to store food and tools and raising their houses on stone foundations. Leaded casement windows had waxed-paper panes until glass became available, and there were often separate front entrances for the hall and the parlor. The cross house—the first Southern manor house—was built on the mid-Atlantic coast from about 1650. This enlarged version of the hall-and-parlor house added a central passage on the ground floor,

accessed by an entry porch, and moved the kitchen into a separate building. A second porch at the back, for the stairwell to the upper rooms, gave the house its cruciform shape. Fireplaces were recessed into the outer walls to conserve space in the newly created dining room and the traditional ground-floor hall—what we would call the living room. Wealthy families built slave quarters above the outside kitchen, which was connected to the main house by an enclosed passage or an open loggia. These houses often had double chimney stacks of the late-medieval kind, which served two fireplaces. Ornamentation was usually limited to flat or round brick arches over windows and doors.

More elaborate cross houses were built in the Early Renaissance style known as Jacobean, imported from England in the seventeenth century. Examples occur in Virginia, Maryland and the Carolinas. They are distinguished by high end walls with stepped or curvilinear gables and massive three-part chimneys serving multiple fireplaces. The best-known Jacobean house on the mid-Atlantic coast was built in Surrey County, Virginia, in 1655 by a newly arrived Englishman named Arthur Allen. It became famous as "Bacon's Castle" when Nathaniel L. Bacon, leader of the 1676 rebellion against Virginia governor Sir William Berkeley, used it to garrison his troops.

The log cabin introduced by the Swedes had many regional variations, including the so-called dogtrot cabin of the southern Appalachians. It had an open breezeway, or "dogtrot," between two cabins with a common roof and outside

Opposite: *Oak Alley (1839), a Greek Revival plantation house near Baton Rouge, Louisiana. The approach, lined by live oaks some 300 years old, gave the stately house its name.*

chimneys at either end. In the vernacular, this style was often called "two pens and a passage," pen being a synonym for cabin. Another variation was the frontier "saddlebag" cabin described in the following chapter.

Once slavery became the basis of the South's plantation economy, one-room slave cabins were built of notched wall logs rising to a gabled roof, with brick fireplaces and chimneys. Most had several windows whose size was determined by the mildness of the climate. These cabins were forerunners of the African-American "shotgun" house, which was developed mainly in the West Indies along central African lines and imported to New Orleans from Haiti early in the nineteenth century.

The shotgun house took its name from its in-line floor plan—usually one room wide and several rooms deep—so that a shot fired from the front door at the gable end would travel straight through the building. The front porches, or verandahs, first seen in the South were also derived from vernacular African architecture: they were extensions of the thatched roof that provided a cool place to gather outside in hot, humid climates. Imported by slaves to the Caribbean and the United States, porches were adopted for frame structures all over the South, and eventually for other dwellings nationwide. In fact, the porch would become a signature of American architecture. Even after the Civil War, many African-American outbuildings retained the thatched roofs of the original style, although houses were roofed with shingles or sheet metal to reflect the heat.

The late 1600s brought new elements to the Southern colonial style, as prosperous merchants and planters increased the size of their houses to show their affluence. Building on the original hall-and-parlor plan, second- and third-generation English colonists added wings to form T-shaped or L-shaped houses. They were sited to face prevailing summer breezes and sometimes had a kitchen wing rather than a separate outbuilding.

The primary construction materials were brick over wood framing, and the two-sloped gambrel roof became increasingly popular—not only here, but in New England as well—because it provided more room upstairs. These roofs were covered with durable split-cedar shingles, and chimneys were located at the gable ends to reduce heat in the summer.

In the early eighteenth century, the South acquired many new residents who had originally immigrated to the North from various European countries. Germans, Scots-Irish, Swiss, French Protestants and others brought their own building traditions, which were reshaped to accommodate new ideas, materials and climatic conditions. German and Scots-Irish emigrants from Pennsylvania introduced the two-story stone house with a symmetrical façade, central hall and twin chimneys at the gable ends. In Virginia and Maryland, this style (later called the "I" house for its popularity in Iowa, Illinois and Indiana) was adapted to frame construction.

Below: *A Cajun house on low-lying ground, modeled on the rural French raised cottage, overlooks a waterway near Nottaway, Louisiana.*

On the Carolina coast, a distinctive cottage style emerged. Based on the hall-and-parlor plan, the frame cottage was raised on stone blocks for air circulation and had lean-tos extending from front and rear—one a porch, the other a bedroom addition. From this time, almost every folk house built in the Deep South would include a south-facing shed porch.

The fashionable port of Charleston, South Carolina, developed a distinctive architectural style influenced by British colonists who came from the West Indies in the late seventeenth century. Wealthy merchants built two- and three-story pastel-colored houses with high-ceilinged rooms. Handsome colonnades and multilevel piazzas were cooled by breezes from historic Charleston Harbor. During the late 1700s, local architects designed many impressive buildings in the Adam style, which the city has preserved with pride to this day.

The Plantation colonial style dominated Southern waterways from the James River to the Mississippi, beginning in the early eighteenth century. They were built by prosperous slave-owners who grew tobacco, rice and, eventually, cotton—all labor-intensive crops transported primarily by riverboat. Land holdings ranged from hundreds to thousands of acres, and planters chose hilltop sites facing the river for coolness. Large overhanging porches were common to several ethnic styles, beginning with the French Huguenot plantation houses of the Carolinas in the 1690s. These two-story houses had in-line rooms with piazzas on both sides to promote cross-ventilation. Characteristically French floor-to-ceiling windows (or French doors) maximized interior light and air.

The nation's best-known plantation house is probably George Washington's Mount Vernon, Virginia, which grew from an original medieval-style English house overlooking the Potomac River, built by Washington's father in the early 1700s, to the national landmark that we see today. During Washington's tenure, it was enlarged repeatedly and ornamented with both Georgian and Adam-style elements. Its two-story columned porch faces the river, and

twin arcades connect the servants' quarters to the main building on the plantation side. Washington's improvements included an elaborate rooftop cupola and an imposing pediment over the main entrance. His early experience as a surveyor, and his consuming interest in both architecture and agriculture, contributed to the stature of this landmark dwelling.

Meanwhile, a distinctive style was emerging in present-day Louisiana and Mississippi, influenced heavily by French settlers. They included the Acadians (called Cajuns) who had been deported from Quebec and Atlantic Canada by the British beginning in 1755. Some 6,000 were shipped to American colonies, where they built houses based on the French colonial raised-cottage model, which incorporated a stone cellar covered with stucco below the main house. Both levels had porchlike galleries on two or more sides to cope with the humid climate, and gabled or hipped roofs. In many cases, double outside staircases provided access to the second floor. French-speaking Creoles from the West Indies left their imprint on this style, especially in New Orleans, the great port situated at the mouth of the Mississippi River.

As Creole planters prospered, their mansions rose along the lower Mississippi delta, financed by sugar cane and cotton. An example is Laura Plantation (1805), near Baton Rouge, Louisiana. Built in the *briquette-entre-poteaux* (brick-between-posts) style, like the contempo-

Above: *Ruins of the old slave cabins at Boone Hall Plantation (1681), near Charleston, South Carolina, where rice was one of the principal crops grown by early settlers.*

Right: *Middleton Place Plantation, near Charleston, is a Jacobean plantation house dating from 1741, recognizable by its curved gables and Early Renaissance detailing.*

raneous New Orleans townhouse, it shows the combined influence of the region's multicultural heritage. More modest houses of French derivation were built by settlers throughout the Mississippi Valley. Originally, the French pioneer house was made of heavy upright logs in the *poteaux-en-terre* (posts-in-earth) style, or the piece-on-piece form of log cabin construction on a timber base. However, since wooden sills at ground level rotted quickly in the damp climate, these cottages were soon raised on pillars of cypress blocks, or stone covered with stucco. They retained the familiar pavilion, or steeply pitched hipped roof, of the French colonial vernacular, but with a sharp break in pitch halfway between the ridgeline and the eaves—the so-called umbrella roof.

The New Orleans townhouse of the late eighteenth century showed its French antecedents in a flared roof, full-length louvered doors, casement windows that could be shuttered in foul weather and sill plates resting on stone foundations. However, the use of Spanish tiles for roofing was adopted as a fire-prevention measure, and brick, inset between timber posts, became a primary construction material. Only much later did the wrought-iron ornamentation associated with the city's French Quarter come into use.

The Regency, last of the Georgian styles to evolve in England, became moderately influen-

tial in the United States from 1815 onward and had its greatest vogue in the South. Transitional between the Adam style and the nationwide Greek Revival, it borrowed from the classical orders of both Greece and Rome. One of its most important American exponents was the architect William Jay, who built several beautiful houses in Savannah that represented the apogee of American neoclassical townhouses. These included the Richardson-Owens-Thomas and the Hull-Barrow Houses (both 1818) and the elegant Telfaire House of 1820. All shared the hallmarks of the Regency style in their classical symmetry, large windows, slender columns, smooth stuccoed walls and curved elements, including Roman arches and niches.

Within a few years, the Greek Revival style had become pre-eminent and would remain so for decades. Believed to embody the ideals of American democracy, it was chosen for the public buildings and mansions of the nation's capital. Soon county courthouses, libraries, schools, churches and private residences were swept up in the tide. Greek elements were borrowed to enhance existing homes, so that after 1830 one could find any number of modest New England and Midwestern farmhouses that had been converted to the fashionable style by the addition of slender wooden columns or a simple pediment at the gable end. Practically everything was painted white to simulate the look of marble.

Architects were engaged to design major public buildings of masonry construction; vernacular buildings were based largely on readily available pattern books and executed in wood. Conservative Southern cities like Baltimore, Richmond, Alexandria and Atlanta took up the style with zeal, and the last of the great prebellum plantation houses, along the lower Mississippi, were heavily influenced by the Greek Revival style. An example is the four-story mansion called Windsor (now in ruins), built by cotton grower Smith Coffee Daniell to the design of architect David Shroder (1859-61).

Originally surrounded by a plantation of more than 2,500 acres near the port of Bruinsburg, Mississippi, Windsor's upper floors, behind their façade of Corinthian columns, contained twenty-three rooms, each with its own fireplace. The basement level included a schoolroom, dairy, dispensary, commissary and numerous store-rooms. A lantern-shaped cupola crowned the roof, and according to Mark Twain, in *Life on the Mississippi*, "the mansion high above the bluffs was visible for miles in every direction." Other examples of the Greek Revival style across the nation are discussed in chapter 4.

Below: *An elegant Charleston townhouse on East Bay Street, with a two-story portico raised on a colonnade. Full-length French windows, elaborate cornices and low balustrades are features of the Charleston style.*

Logs, Lean-tos and "Dogtrot" Cabins

The Kentucky cabin at far left has a brick chimney and masonry infill between the squared-off logs. The attic story is built of boards. At top left is a vernacular gabled house with a lean-to addition in Old Salem, North Carolina. Lean-tos and porches are characteristic of Southern architecture.

"Dogtrot" cabins like the one pictured above—actually two cabins with a breezeway between them and a common roof— were once a common sight in the South. Sometimes the settler used the second cabin to shelter livestock until a barn could be constructed.

Creole and Caribbean Influence

The board cottages raised on brick piers, at right, have been preserved from the 1800s at Acadian Village in Lafayette, Louisiana. They exemplify the Cajun cottages built along the state's many bayous by French settlers deported from Atlantic Canada at the onset of the Seven Years' War in 1755. The ubiquitous Southern porch (below) soon spread across the country as a desirable extension of common living space in mild or seasonal climates. The example opposite, below, is from the resort of Cape May, New Jersey.

Mansions and Main Streets

Affluent Southerners proclaimed their success with elegant townhouses like those designed in post-Revolutionary Charleston (above) by architect Gabriel Manigault. A later example (opposite, top) is the French Empire-style house built for John Bremond, Jr., in Austin, Texas (1886), which also has the region's elegant columned piazzas at both levels to alleviate the heat. A typical nineteenth-century downtown area (right) shows a "Rainbow Row" of pastel Italianate townhouses with flat roofs defined by prominent cornices and arched windows, both single and paired.

The Greek Revival—Southern Style

This style was especially popular in the South, as seen in these handsome examples with Victorian ornamentation. At left is a two-story New Orleans townhouse with an ornate and unusual rooftop pediment and second-story cast-iron balustrade that echoes the decorative fencing. This theme is reprised on the opposite page in an impressive New Orleans house with both Ionic (ground floor) and Corinthian columns. Below is the Hamilton-Phinizy-Segrest House (1858), with lacy ironwork and a curved double-stairway approach, in the university town of Athens, Georgia.

Mississippi Delta Plantation Houses

As pre-Civil War agriculture flourished, planters moved farther west and built their comfortable country houses according to regional needs and fashions. These three are from the delta's "Cotton Kingdom" era and show the prevailing Greek Revival influence. Above, Weymouth Hall (1855) in Natchez, Mississippi, famous for its beautiful homes; opposite, top, St. Emma Plantation (1850) near Belle Rose, Louisiana; right, Mintmere Plantation (1850) in New Iberia, Louisiana, raised on piers in the French manner to prevent flooding and the deterioration of wooden sills installed at the marshy ground level.

The Long Reign of Classicism

The South's long love affair with neoclassical styles began with the Georgian, as seen below in Drayton Hall, near Charleston (1742). The architect of this brick country house with Palladian detailing is unknown, but his work has been safeguarded by the National Trust for Historic Preservation.

A century later, Melrose (opposite, top) was erected in Greek Revival splendor along the Mississippi, at the rich port of Natchez. The symmetrical façade of the later plantation house below, near Washington State Park, retains the paired elements and restrained ornamentation of its predecessors.

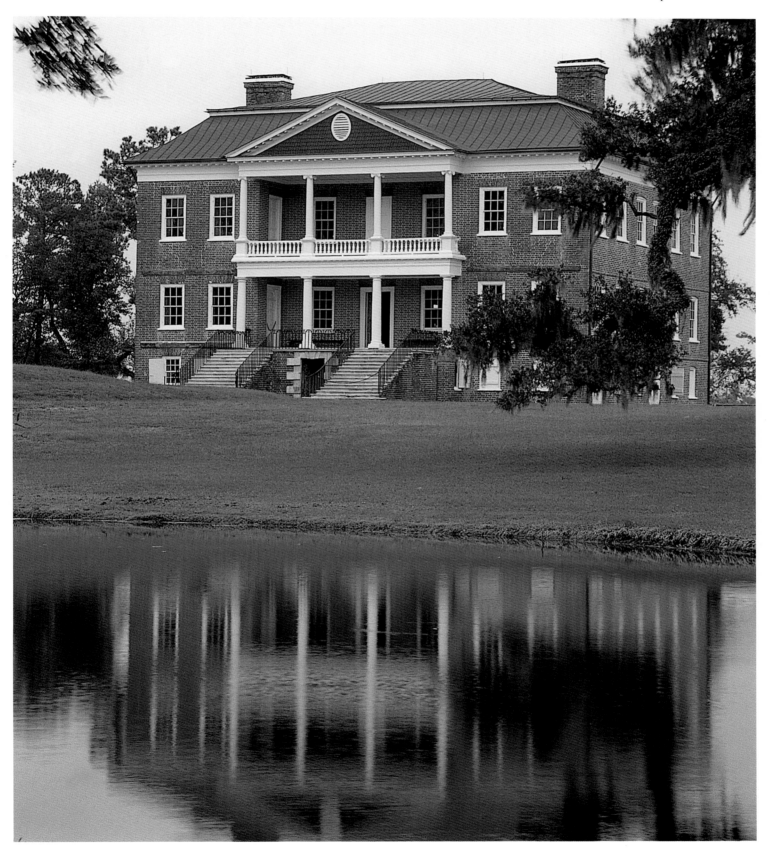

Frontier and Heartland Vernacular Styles

As mentioned in earlier chapters, a number of log building styles were used on both the American and Canadian frontiers for some 300 years, leaving their imprint on regional architecture from the Delaware Valley to the Canadian prairie provinces. By 1740, in the Ohio River Valley, the original one-room log cabin had been enlarged to two rooms with a central fireplace. Called the "saddlebag" cabin, apparently because the rooms overhung the fireplace on either side, this pioneer dwelling shared the advantages of its predecessors. It was readily constructed from materials at hand and provided natural insulation with its thick wooden walls, chinked with mud or clay.

In *America's Architectural Roots*, historian Lena Aison Palmquist observes that "The American saddlebag house with two rooms and a central chimney is probably derived from the Swedish *stuga av celltyp* (cell-type cottage). Both Swedish and American saddlebag houses have two front doors, a shed porch and two rooms of approximately equal size. The Fenno-Scandinavian gatehouse, known in Sweden as a *portlider*, is quite similar to the dogtrot house of the Delaware area."

By the late eighteenth century, pioneers in Kentucky were building two- and three-story log cabins, with two bedrooms on the second floor, each with its own staircase. Tiny square windows in the attic provided minimal light and ventilation. The gable roof might extend from one end to shelter a second-story porch and an outside stairway to the storage cellar.

The impetus of westward migration during the nineteenth century saw new styles of log-cabin construction, especially on the mining and lumber frontiers. In Michigan, the single-room lumberjack's cabin was heated by a wood-burning stove whose metal chimney was strapped to the outside wall. Rounded roof logs were designed to shed rain. Colorado miners also used wood stoves with tin chimneys; their roof boards were overlapped and caulked with dry grass or moss for insulation. In some cases, notched wall logs were extended to form porch walls with an open gable above for air circulation.

Many German settlers arrived in the Midwest during the nineteenth century, bringing their characteristic *Fachwerk*, or half-timber, building style. Their dwellings are more properly called log houses than cabins. The framework of braced timbers was filled in (nogged) with brick or clay—a method native to Pomerania, Saxony and other Prussian areas. Examples have been preserved in the museum village at Old World Wisconsin, in the town of Eagle. German settlers also built a number of house-barns in their traditional style, and they often arranged their outbuildings—stone smokehouses, ovens and livestock shelters—around a three-sided courtyard. This type of grouping, called "continuous architecture," was also used by French settlers from Normandy who emigrated to eastern Canada and the Mississippi Valley.

Several Utopian settlements were formed by Germans in the Midwest, including New Harmony, Indiana, and Iowa's Amana colonies.

Opposite: *A second-generation log house with shingled roof and brick chimney, built near Dallas, Texas, in the mid-1800s.*

Like the Shaker and Amish communities farther east, they built simple communal houses surrounded by fields, kitchen gardens and workshops designed to make their settlements self-supporting. While the Amish worshipped in their own homes, the Amana, Mennonite and other Utopian colonies were generally clustered around a rustic church with minimal ornamentation, similar to the Quaker meetinghouse.

Belgian immigrants to the Lake Michigan region built farmhouses of red brick over log framing, beginning about the late 1850s. Concentrated in Wisconsin, Michigan and Illinois, they began to import light Cream City brick from Milwaukee to form decorative door and window surrounds and ornamental gables. Skilled masons traveled from farm to farm to do this work, leaving a circular or half-moon window in the front-facing gable as a kind of signature. The Belgian-American farmhouse was also identified by its outdoor summer kitchen and roofed-over bake oven attached to the house. Dairy farming was the main occupation, and Belgian settlers prospered through their careful husbandry and the abundance of well-watered pasturage in Wisconsin's Door Peninsula and adjacent areas.

Irish immigrants brought the original Celtic-style cottage, consisting of two rooms with a fireplace at one end and a thatched roof. This plan was modified to both log and masonry construction, with the addition of a second-story loft accessed by a stairway. Irish, English and German traditions merged in both rural and urban areas, as seen in working-class rowhouses like those preserved in the Philadelphia neighborhood called "the Pocket." These terraced brick houses are almost identical, ornamented only by white cornices and steps that recall the traditional whitewash of the Celtic cottage. Similar rowhouses were built in Boston and other cities that experienced heavy Irish immigration during the 1800s.

Norwegian families began to arrive in the Middle West about 1825, and the houses they built reflected medieval archetypes. Early single-room examples had an off-center entrance in the gable end. Both frame and log were used

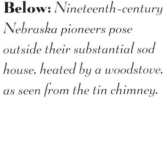

Below: *Nineteenth-century Nebraska pioneers pose outside their substantial sod house, heated by a woodstove, as seen from the tin chimney.*

for construction, with a moderately pitched roof. Eventually, many log houses in the heartland were covered with weatherboards, as sawmills were built to provide precut lumber. The sod roof common in Scandinavia was replaced by wooden shingles, except on the Great Plains, where wood was in short supply. Siding was most often painted white. Like the German settlers of Pennsylvania, the Norwegians often constructed banked barns, partly dug into a hillside for insulation and accessed by an earthen ramp.

Most of the original Danish immigrants of the nineteenth century were Mormon converts who had been visited by missionaries from Salt Lake City, Utah. Most settled there first, then spread into the upper Midwest. Their architecture was based on several different European models, including masonry houses with gabled roofs and twin chimneys, and the Danish-style country house, with a hipped roof and segmental hood molds over the windows. Anglo-American influence was seen in their frame houses with central passageways and a prominent dormer over the main entrance.

Settlement of the Great Plains began during the mid-nineteenth century with pioneers from the East Coast and many ethnic groups from Europe. On the plains, deep soil covered the rock that could have served as building stone, so special plows were developed to cut the topsoil, with its thick grass roots, into building blocks. Sod shelters were often built over partial dugouts, with timber framing for the doorways. The walls provided good insulation against the bitter Plains winters, but sod roofs often leaked during heavy rains. Over time, frame extensions were added to form various T-shaped and L-shaped plans adjacent to sod outbuildings and livestock shelters.

During the 1890s, many Ukrainian settlers came to the Canadian prairie provinces of Manitoba, Saskatchewan and Alberta. Their native architecture was of log construction, with gabled or hipped roofs; the exteriors were often whitewashed with lime. The interior walls were plastered with mud and straw.

Some Ukrainians, and many other immigrants from northern Europe, settled in the Dakotas at a time when the U.S. railway system was nearing completion. This national transportation network would have a far-reaching effect on architecture. Both building materials and styles were more widely disseminated than ever before, and provincial models were adapted to reflect the new trends that are discussed in chapters 4 and 5. Eventually, the typical Midwestern community would consist of rectangular, two-story brick or frame houses that might be ornamented in a variety of fashionable styles, from Greek Revival to the Gothic and Italianate styles. As one contemporary writer observed before the turn of the century, "Not even the cholera is so contagious in this country as the style of architecture which we happen to catch."

Above: *This timeworn farmhouse in Mankota, Saskatchewan, clad in weatherboard, once sheltered immigrants to the vast region opened for settlement by the emergence of the Canadian Pacific Railway, completed in 1885.*

Southwestern Pueblo Construction

Native American builders have employed both adobe brick and puddled adobe (wet clay) surfacing over timber framing since ancient times. Pueblo villagers still use ladders to access their flat roofs and second-story apartments, as seen below at Taos (left) and Acoma (right), New Mexico. Spanish settlers from Mexico adopted this style for farmsteads like El Rancho de Las Golondrinas, at left.

Ethnic Frontier Folkhouses

On the opposite page, the ruins of a masonry pioneer house with a double entry are surrounded by flowering bluebonnets and Indian blankets along a Texas byway. At right (above) is the first house built by a Polish community in Panna Maria, Texas, with the roof extended to form a front porch supported by posts. Below it are an African house with a wide-eaved hip roof (originally thatched) at Louisiana's Melrose Plantation, and a log cabin with fieldstone chimney from the old slave quarter at Raytown, Missouri (1837).

Adaptations in Log Construction

These nineteenth-century log houses reflect advances upon
the original Swedish log cabins of the 1600s. Brick and
fieldstone chimneys replaced the original mud-lined stick
chimneys that posed a constant fire hazard. Second stories,
porches and lean-tos were added for more living space, and
hard-packed dirt floors were replaced by board flooring.
These examples are from the West except the building at top
right, at the Utopian community of New Harmony, Indiana.
The double log cabin below (1836) is preserved in Old Baylor
Park, Independence, Texas.

Southwest and Southeast

The Joseph Bird House, right, is a second-generation log dwelling with a full-length porch, twin chimneys and a dormer window, built in 1858 near Round Mountain, Texas. Split-rail fencing surrounds the property, and machine-made shingles have replaced the laboriously hand-split shingles of an earlier day. Below is a late nineteenth-century frame farmhouse near Julietta, Georgia, built by Richard Jarrell and maintained by the Jarrell Plantation State Historic Park.

Prosperous Western Homesteads

The handsome Brandenberger Ranch House (below), in Mason County, Texas, testifies to the rapid growth of the "Cattle Kingdom" with the arrival of railheads to Eastern markets. The two-story fieldstone Ellerbracht farmstead (opposite) commands a view of flowering fields and nearby Threadgill Creek, in Mason County. At right is a German-style farmhouse in Mineral Point, Wisconsin, combining masonry and log construction.

New Styles in the Heartland

Clean lines and ample windows mark the spacious frame farmhouse at left, in Wisconsin, which was settled principally by German immigrants attracted by the region's rich soil and pastureland. Below it is an historic ranch house in the Gothic Revival mode near Carson City, Nevada, which became a prosperous mining center during the 1800s. On the opposite page, an elegant pagoda-style roofline and Italianate window moldings distinguish a Victorian-era house designed by a young builder in Kalamazoo, Michigan, for his family.

Midwestern Medieval and Italianate Inspiration

The landmark Heritage Hill House in Grand Rapids, Michigan, at right, shows the influence of the Tudor Revival, with a brickwork ground floor surmounted by half-timbering with stucco infill and casement windows at the second-story level. The attractive Italianate house on the opposite page, with double brackets along the cornice line, was built after the Civil War in Bloomfield, Michigan. Below is a Tudor-style brick house with steep front-facing gables and a massive chimney in Genoa, Wisconsin. Note the flattened Tudor arch that frames the doorway. This style became immensely popular at the turn of the century, and examples are found across the United States and Canada.

Classical and Gothic Revivals

As seen in chapter 2, the Greek Revival style first became popular in the South, as a result of the mansions and public buildings of Washington, D.C. From about 1820 onward, it spread rapidly, with most of the original buildings designed by architects, who adhered closely to the Greek orders: columns with shafts, capitals, entablatures and, in most cases, bases. The style became increasingly popular, as an emblem of democratic ideals and civic virtue, and local masons and carpenters learned how to execute its detailing in wood, plaster and other materials less expensive than cut stone.

Hallmarks of the Greek Revival house (often adapted from an earlier style) include a wide band of trim below the eaves resembling a Greek entablature; a low-pitched roof; entry porches with columns; and orientation of the gable end toward the street, recalling the façade of the Greek temple. Among the architects who were instrumental in popularizing the style were Benjamin Latrobe, whose Bank of Pennsylvania in Philadelphia (1801) was the first Greek Revival building in the United States; Robert Mills and James Hoban, who designed many buildings in the nation's capital, including the National Portrait Gallery, formerly the U.S. Patent Office (1840); and Thomas Jefferson, whose Monticello, in its final form, owes much to the influence of Latrobe.

The Greek Revival style appeared in Canada during the 1820s and remained popular for about thirty years. Generally called the Neoclassical style, it reflected the growing interest in ancient classical models as discovered in Greece and Italy by European archaeologists of the late eighteenth century. The original buildings had proved to differ in several ways from the derivative Renaissance classical styles, being simpler, bolder and more blocklike in form. As interpreted by Canadian architects, Greek Revival detailing included Greek and Roman columns, especially the Ionic and Doric orders; Greek fretwork and key designs; acanthus leaves; elliptical fanlights; and parapets or balustrades along a low-pitched roofline.

Few buildings carried out the Greek temple theme in its entirety, that is, a rectangular building with colonnades on all four sides. Most examples had a colonnade only along the façade. House plans were symmetrical, with the rooms opening from a central hall, and decorative

Opposite: *The imposing Neoclassical Lanier House in Madison, Wisconsin, built in the late 1800s, has a two-story portico on a masonry base and a low balustrade of ornamental ironwork. The ornament above the roofline is an acroterion.*

Below: *Both Neoclassical and Gothic elements are seen in the former Levi Morton schoolhouse in Rhinecliff, New York, with its prominent dentils along the roofline and cornices and vertical board-and-batten siding.*

Above: *Wood Farm is a picturesque Midwestern Gothic cottage with unusual pointed windows and shutters and a shingle roof patterned in the style of the late nineteenth century.*

details included small columns or pilasters in fireplace surrounds, cornices inspired by classical models, fretwork, key designs and ceiling rosettes with acanthus leaves or other botanical ornamentation.

As in the United States, this classical style was widely used for public buildings in a country experiencing rapid growth: courthouses, schools, post offices, colleges and city halls. Architectural pattern books brought the Greek Revival to vernacular architecture primarily in the form of details like pediments and pilasters added to existing houses, as seen in Halifax, Nova Scotia, and in other Atlantic provinces. When used for mansions like Rockwood Villa in Kingston, Ontario (George Browne, architect, 1841), it took the form of stone, brick, or stucco, with simple moldings around the windows and a portico several stories high, with the entrance inset behind it. Canadian townhouses of the period were designed in a similar manner, except that the door was usually to one side and ornamented by sidelights or pilasters under an arched opening.

As the authors of *A Guide to Canadian Architectural Styles* (Broadview Press, 1992) point out: "The impact of historicism varied considerably within Canada, whose far-flung regions, each with its own climatic conditions and building materials, had developed strong traditions of their own. In Atlantic Canada, for example, classicism and the traditions of wood construction remained important factors. Thus, many charming vernacular versions of the high

styles were developed using wood as the principal material and manifesting the underlying persistence of classicism. In Quebec, the vigorous survival of a two-hundred-year-old building tradition, which included a distinct domestic and religious form of architecture, ensured that that province's nineteenth-century architecture possessed characteristics not found elsewhere in the country.... The Prairie provinces were settled later in the century, and their architecture reflected the limitations of pioneering settlement. British Columbia was a slightly older colony [whose] milder climate, English traditions, and cultural connections with the American West Coast made for a distinctive and sometimes flamboyant architecture."

Few Greek Revival houses were built in New England before the 1830s. The established Federal style did not lend itself to conversion except in the form of a modest Doric porch, perhaps a small pediment and friezelike detailing under the eaves. However, once the Greek Revival swept all before it, some sturdy New Englanders did a complete about-face and redesigned their houses so that the gable end faced the street, complete with pediment and columns. This often entailed an addition to the basic colonial house and a new floor plan, with an entrance hall on one side and a single row of connecting rooms on the other.

A decade or so later, the Greek Revival made itself felt in the Midwest in the form of a recessed porch with Doric columns and wooden-pilaster trimwork at the corners of the house. A substantial Michigan or Illinois farmhouse of this type might have a parlor to one side of the front entrance, a large living room, three or more bedrooms, kitchen with pantry and a spacious back porch for relaxation and family gatherings. Before its popularity waned, the style had reached the West Coast with the gold rush of the mid-century, although it was never as influential there as it had been in other parts of the country, especially the South.

Meanwhile, a formidable competitor was rising on the East Coast in the form of the early Gothic Revival style. It had begun in England during the early 1800s and was popularized in the United States by architect Alexander Jackson Davis and his friend and colleague Andrew Jackson Downing, a landscape architect and writer. Deeply influenced by the work of England's John Ruskin and Augustus Pugin, they took elements from the late Gothic manor house, with its asymmetrical form and picturesque details including battlements and turrets, and translated them first into stone, for wealthy clients, and later into wood, for affordable middle-class housing. Davis produced the nation's first house-plan book, *Rural Residences,* in 1837, with three-dimensional views and floor plans. Downing's influential books, including *Cottage Residences* (1842) and *The Architecture of Country Houses* (1850), inspired countless pattern books providing detailed plans in the American Gothic mode.

An early example of the style is A.J. Davis's mansion Lyndhurst, in Tarrytown, New York (1842). Its elegant flush-cut stone walls and pinnacles, with carved tracery borrowed from medieval castles and cathedrals, were much admired, and its meandering floor plan con-

formed to the lay of the land and the owner's preferences rather than to rigidly prescribed conventions. Inspired by Downing's *Cottage Residences,* those who could not afford an architect soon combined picturesque elements of the style in wooden houses like the one built by Justin Smith Morrill in Vermont, in 1850. Pale beige siding replaced cut stone, and carved bargeboards under the gable ends—soon to be known as "gingerbread" trim—took the place of expensive stone tracery. Long narrow windows and a steep roof with thin chimneys emphasized the vertical. Prototypes like this soon inspired the widely disseminated Carpenter Gothic style, with the help of rapidly constructed balloon framing and steam-powered scroll saws. The introduction of balloon framing during the 1840s meant that a continuous framework of light wooden members could be assembled with machine-made nails seemingly overnight, in contrast to the laborious post-and-beam method of traditional architecture. The method's low cost, ease of construction and strength made it especially popular in the rapidly expanding Midwest and Far West.

Below: *The ornate Carpenter Gothic style reached new heights in the Midwest, as seen in this polychrome mansion with multiple steep gables crowned by strong finials.*

Right: *An unusual Octagon house in Rhode Island displays a large cupola, used to light and ventilate the interior, and bracketed cornice lines. The exterior of such an eight-sided house could be articulated in almost any style, and many examples were built during the 1860s from such popular manuals as* The American Cottage Builder.

The Carpenter Gothic house could be readily enlarged because of the variety of shapes comprising it, so it grew with the needs of a growing family. Vertical board-and-batten siding, trellised porch columns for climbing plants, ornate chimney stacks and rooftop finials added to the charm of this picturesque style. Carpenters based their ornamental woodwork on natural forms like vines, flowers, waves and the rising sun—motifs that appeared on everything from porch brackets to balustrades and window frames. As with the Greek Revival style, many vernacular houses were updated to conform to the new fashion.

An especially flamboyant form of this indigenous style is known as Steamboat Gothic, because it was used to ornament the paddlewheel riverboats that plied the Ohio and Mississippi Rivers. Houses in this style often had scroll-sawn roof ridges that resembled iron crestwork, jig-sawn gable ornamentation and rich interiors glowing with burnished woodwork and elegant drapery and carpets. Examples include the Mark Twain House in Hartford, Connecticut, where the great American humorist wrote several of his classics, and the Wedding Cake House in Kennebunkport, Maine (1854).

Another variation on the picturesque was the Italianate style, which flourished between 1840 and 1885. It was inspired by the historic villas and townhouses of Italy and took several basic forms in American architecture: the square-towered Tuscan Villa and the Italianate townhouse, of which the urban brownstone is an example. The country house, or villa type, was usually two or three stories high, with a square tower or cupola surmounting a low-pitched roof or rising from the intersection of an L-shaped plan. Wide eaves were supported by evenly spaced decorative brackets. These houses had tall, narrow arched windows, often paired, or ranked in threes along the façade above the doorway.

The Italianate townhouse had wide projecting cornices with brackets and a flat or low-pitched roof. (This form was also popular for commercial buildings.) Some townhouses had a square tower centered on or alongside the façade; others had bay windows, often hooded and framed. After 1860 cast-iron tracery was also used for ornamental detailing. Many variations on the Italianate style were adopted for the Victorian mansions and folk houses described in the following chapter.

Less popular was the restrained and expensive Renaissance Revival style, which recalled the ducal palaces of Renaissance Rome and Florence. It was usually constructed of smooth cut-stone blocks that contrasted with rough-cut ornamental quoins at the corners of the building. Closely spaced windows varied in design from one level to another, and the symmetrical façade featured sixteenth-century colonnades at the main entrance, often reprised by paired arches on the second-story level. American architects who had studied in France at the renowned *École des Beaux Arts* practiced this eclectic use of classical forms, including those of ancient Greece and Rome, Renaissance Italy and eighteenth-century European Neoclassicism. Several examples are seen in Newport, Rhode Island, a fashionable summer place for wealthy Americans like Cornelius Vanderbilt. His residence, The Breakers, was designed by the distinguished architect Richard Morris Hunt in 1896.

In Canada, the Beaux-Arts style influenced many architects through such illustrated journals as *Canadian Architect and Builder*. Others turned to the Edwardian Classical style, imported by British-trained architects who sought to solidify Canada's British ties through the use of English baroque and classical forms adopted during the reign of King Edward VII at the turn of the century. Many public buildings were constructed in this style, including Regina's Saskatchewan Legislative Building, designed by the Montreal architects E. and W.S. Maxwell. Other Canadian architects sought to combine the best features of the Beaux-Arts and Edwardian Classical styles.

The famous Universal Exposition held in Chicago in 1893 was dominated by the Beaux-Arts style and created its own Neoclassical Revival, based on Georgian models but distinct in style. Later called generically "Colonial," houses in the Georgian Revival style were larger than their prototypes, with extensive dormers and porches in the Victorian mode, but a simple rectangular plan with minimal projections and a balanced façade. Both hipped and gambrel roofs were used. The style was popularized by the prestigious East Coast firm of McKim, Mead, and White and ranged from their elegant Taylor House in Newport (1885) to simpler turn-of-the-century vernacular versions with clapboard siding and an oversized dormer on the gable end facing the street. This and other revival styles described here reappear in new guises in the following chapter.

Below: *A substantial stone house in the asymmetrical Gothic Revival style in Greenfield Village, Michigan. Note the extended lintel supported on brackets over the doorway to protect the entrance, much like the pent roofs seen on Pennsylvania Dutch farmhouses.*

Greek Revival, North and South

The Greek Revival style got a late start in the northern United States vis-a-vis the South, but it took hold in the 1830s with property owners who could afford professional architects. On the opposite page is an elegant example from Southport, Connecticut, with Adam-style detailing in the pediment and fluted columns. The house has both shutters and sidelights on the façade inset behind its two-story portico. At left is an 1840s mansion in Red Hook, New York, with decorative circular windows in the pediment. A classic Franklin touring car adds a distinctive touch to this fine country house. Above is elegant Stanton Hall, in Natchez, Mississippi, with distinctively Southern wrought ironwork ornamenting the front elevation.

Prebellum Plantations

Macon, Georgia, is the site of two of these impressive
plantation houses: the Woodruff House (above), built in
1836, and the Scott-Johnston House (opposite, top), from the
mid-1840s. Both have full-height wraparound porticoes in
the true Greek temple style, although the integrity of the
latter house is compromised by the boxlike extension at the
back. Porticoes that extended around three sides of the house
were seldom seen. Opposite, below, is Dunleith, in Natchez,
Mississippi, with plain, slender columns on prominent bases.
Full-length French windows along the galleries provide
ventilation in the sultry Mississippi delta climate. Such
manor houses were always built facing the river, to take
advantage of cooling breezes.

Eclectic Southern Mansions

Greek and Gothic Revivals merge at Walter Place (opposite, top), in Holly Springs, Mississippi, built in 1859. The fan-lighted Greek pediment is flanked by twin bays crowned with battlements in the medieval manner. Opposite, below, is Hay House in, Macon, Georgia, built in the late 1850s. It combines Italianate inspiration with Greek Revival detailing at the entryway and elaborate Gothic chimneys.

Longwood, above, in Natchez, Mississippi, is an octagonal house designed in 1860 by architect Samuel Sloan for Haller Nutt, who died soon after, during the Civil War. The bulb-shaped dome on the rooftop belvedere is an exotic feature that contained mirrors to reflect sunlight into the four-story central hall. The ornate mansion, which some called "Nutt's Folly," was never finished because of the war.

Mid-century Gothic Revival

Lyndhurst (1842), on the opposite page, was designed for Philip R. Paulding by architect Alexander Jackson Davis, an apostle of the American Gothic style. Built in Tarrytown, New York, it was his major residential commission. An addition was designed for George Merritt in 1867, retaining the flush-cut stone walls and pinnacles of the original. Graceful towers, steep gables, corner quoins and decorative ironwork distinguish the Lockwood-Mathews mansion, now a museum, in coastal Norwalk, Connecticut. Note the pointed "candle-snuffer" tower roofs reminiscent of the French chateau. The slender columns of the irregular porchline contribute to the beauty of this historic house.

Carpenter's Gothic

Countless picturesque houses like these were executed in wood by skillful American and Canadian carpenters working from pattern books. Scroll-sawn "gingerbread" trim was substituted for expensive stone tracery. Opposite is the Joseph Hall House (1868) in Cape May, New Jersey, with the community's most striking color combinations—mustard yellow and blue—and an intricately carved vergeboard, or bargeboard, on the front-facing gable. Below is the charming Yeo House in Green Park Provincial Park, on Canada's Prince Edward Island, and at right is the Hyde House in Hydeville, Vermont.

Italianate and French Empire

After the Civil War, the fashionable Italianate and French Empire styles vied for popular supremacy and were often combined, as seen in the mansard rooflines and hooded dormers of the Gallagher House (opposite) in Cape May, New Jersey, and Beaconsfield (below), in Charlottetown, Prince Edward Island, which is crowned by an Italianate cupola. At left is a rambling Western farmhouse that has been decked out with Italianate bracketing, lavish gingerbread trim and quoinlike detailing at the corners, located in Ferndale, California.

Eclectic Turn-of-the-Century Houses

Glen Auburn (opposite), on Natchez, Mississippi's, South Commerce Street, was the home of Simon Moses, one of the city's successful Jewish businessmen, whose commercial establishments lined busy Main and Franklin Streets. Below is the Moran-Durflinger House (1870) in Mason, Texas, which combines Renaissance detailing and plantation-house features. The Italianate house at right, in the style often described as American Bracketed Villa, is one of Cape May, New Jersey's, many outstanding homes. The entire town has been designated a National Historic Landmark.

Picturesque and Neoclassical Features

On the opposite page is a brick house in the popular Tuscan-villa style, with a square tower where the wings intersect. Built in Monroe, Michigan, it has single and double window crowns of inverted U-shape. At right is the Italianate Lehigh Mansion in Clinton, New Jersey, built in the cubic townhouse form with the addition of a columned porch. The Wellington, Ohio, house below is Georgian in form, with symmetrical arched windows crowned by keystones in the façade. The broken pediment at the roofline is a Greek-Revival feature, and the bracketed eaves and entryway reflect Italianate influence.

Victorian Villas, Estates and Townhouses

The period just before and after the Civil War brought many innovations to North American architecture—so many that eclecticism may be called the hallmark of the period. As prosperity increased, people became more concerned with the beauty of their homes and with creating an ideal environment for their families and communities. This sentiment drew inspiration from the Garden Suburb movement in Great Britain, which called for attractive and healthful homes as the sign of a well-ordered society, and was fostered in the United States by theorists like Orson S. Fowler and the redoubtable team of A.J. Davis and A.J. Downing. They gave new meaning to the phrase "A man's home is his castle," and proved it by producing copious house plans on which owner and builder could collaborate without the expense of a professional architect.

Exotic new forms were inspired by Egyptian, Oriental and other models imported from the Far East by way of Europe. Suburban villas sprouted onion-shaped domes, ogee (S-curve) arches and geometric patterns in masonry ornamentation. Alexander J. Davis designed the Apthorp House in New Haven, Connecticut, in the Egyptian style, as seen in the form of massive fluted columns flared at the top. The best-known example of the Exotic style is the Hudson River Valley estate Olana, designed by landscape painter Frederick E. Church in 1874 with

Opposite: *This Heritage Home in Twillingate, Newfoundland, is a sturdy Atlantic Canadian farmhouse brought up to date by Victorian two-story bays with conical tower roofs, and a full-width front porch with decorative woodwork on a latticework base.*

Left: *This colorful cottage with a wealth of detailing was built by Texas congressman George Burgess in Gonzales at the turn of the century. Note the variety of window styles and the entry-porch roof that slopes out over the stairs on one side.*

Above: *A roomy, rambling Queen Anne house in coastal Rowayton, Connecticut, has a square tower where two wings intersect and full-length bay windows along the façade. Exterior banding marks the various levels, which are patterned with clapboards and shingles.*

the help of architect Calvert Vaux, who was instrumental in creating New York City's Central Park. Church's dream house was realized in Olana, with its multilevel roofline, fanciful towers, elegant archways and Moorish detailing. A few years later, the J.M. Carson house in Eureka, California, took the mysterious East to new heights by combining an onion-shaped dome with lacy balustrades, finials, an elaborate gable ornament and other features of the reigning Queen Anne Revival style.

Another essay into the picturesque was the Swiss Chalet style, recommended by A.J. Downing for "bold and mountainous sites." This type of country house is recognized by its low-pitched, front-gabled roof and wide eaves. It has a second-story porch or balcony with a flat cut-out balustrade and trim. Some versions featured patterned stickwork on exterior walls. A.J. Davis designed a house in this style near Tarrytown, New York, in 1867, and examples are still seen in the northern United States, although Swiss cottagers of the early nineteenth century might have had difficulty recognizing them. Their pro-

totypes were two-story folk houses in which the first floor housed farm animals.

Rarely seen now, the Octagon house was popularized by lecturer Orson S. Fowler in 1849, when he published a pattern book entitled *A Home for All, or the Gravel Wall and Octagon Mode of Building.* His theory was that this unusual shape provided better light and ventilation (through a central cupola) than the conventional square house. Hygiene was one of his main concerns, and he incorporated many modern conveniences into the house he built for himself in Fishkill, New York (1850). They included hot and cold running water, filtered drinking water, dumb waiters and flush toilets. Long after the octagon-shaped house had its brief day in the sun, these improvements had become standard in new housing construction.

The indigenous Stick style became fashionable on the East Coast after the publication in 1858 of A.J. Downing's *Architecture of Country Carpentry Made Easy.* This picturesque style was transitional between the Gothic Revival and the Queen Anne, both of which also featured adaptations of medieval English designs. It was sometimes called the Eastlake style, for the English furniture designer Charles Eastlake, who advocated similar ornamentation in his interiors. Wall surfaces were patterned with horizontal, vertical and diagonal boards called stickwork. Decorative trusses were used as gable ornaments, and porches had curving support brackets. Stick-style houses had steeply pitched gabled roofs, wide eaves with brackets and wall cladding of shingles or clapboard alternating with the raised stickwork. Townhouse versions had a flat roof rather than a pitched roof, as seen in San Francisco, where the style became popular during the 1870s in the midst of a building boom that favored wooden construction because of the West Coast's abundant lumber.

After the Civil War, the Second Empire style became extremely popular nationwide. It was imported from France by way of England during the reign of Napoleon III (1852–70). The emperor undertook to transform Paris into a city of huge tree-lined boulevards and monumental buildings, including the new Louvre (1852–57). Its style combined French Renaissance and classical French architecture and its influence was widely felt.

The most distinctive feature of the style is the mansard roof—a dual-pitched hipped roof with dormer windows on the steep lower slope. Other elements included molded cornices along the lower roofline and decorative brackets below the eaves, as seen in the contemporaneous Italianate style.

On the Second Empire house, the windows were usually ranked in threes, with elaborate surrounds. Paired entry doors and one- or two-story porches with balustrades were characteristic. Some examples had decorative cupolas with mansard roofs and small dormers. The style was popular for townhouses because it provided an extra story behind the roofline, which increased interior space on the comparatively narrow city lot. Decorative iron cresting often added an elegant touch to the roofline.

The mansard roof (named for the seventeenth-century French architect François

Mansart) was varied in several ways, especially when added to a pre-Victorian building. It could be straight-sided, or have either a concave or a convex arc. Sometimes the two were combined to form an S-shaped curve. Americans considered the style very up-to-date, and it became so popular after the Civil War that it was sometimes called the General Grant style, for the military hero who served two terms as president, from 1869 to 1877.

Not surprisingly, this style also became popular in Canada, shortly after it was adopted in the United States. The most elaborate examples occur in churches and government buildings, but a modified version of the style was used for domestic architecture. Second Empire houses became fashionable all over the country for some twenty years: they are especially prevalent in

Below: *A High Victorian-era townhouse in Montreal combines Gothic and French Empire detailing with smooth and rusticated masonry at the ground-floor level. The upper story was almost certainly remodeled in the late nineteenth century.*

St. John's, Newfoundland; St. John, New Brunswick; and the old province of Quebec. Ontario also has handsome examples of the style, including the two-story house at 201 Charles Street in Belleville, which was constructed of light-colored brick with a patterned slate roof and lavish Victorian ornamentation.

About 1875 the style known as High Victorian Gothic emerged, influenced by the writings of the British cultural historian John Ruskin. His major works included *The Seven Lamps of Architecture* and *The Stones of Venice*. This style was based largely on medieval models from northern Italy rather than from English roots, as in the earlier Gothic Revival. Ruskin's *The Seven Lamps of Architecture* advocated a new basis for the use of color in buildings, known

as polychrome. Rather than applied color, like paint, it should be intrinsic to the construction materials, whether stone, slate, multicolored brick, or a patterned combination of such materials. Decorative bands, called stringcourses, defined the various levels and emphasized corners and arches. Where masonry could not be used, board siding was painted to resemble stonework, and heavy trimwork was used in lieu of expensive carved stone. Roofing was made from bands of differently colored slate tiles, and narrow towers with conical roofs in the same mode contributed to the vertical thrust of the building, enhanced by rooftop finials.

Clearly, the High Victorian Gothic style figured largely in the Queen Anne Revival, which became the dominant style in domestic architecture after the Philadelphia Centennial of 1876. This most eclectic of the nineteenth-century styles combined medieval and classical motifs borrowed from English architecture during the reign of Queen Anne, some 150 years earlier. It emphasized solid craftsmanship and was popularized in England by the late work of architect Richard Norman Shaw. Medieval elements included Tudor windows, corner towers, ornate chimney pots, bay and oriel windows and carving. From the classical realm came such features as columns and pilasters, pediments and arched Palladian windows.

The Queen Anne style was adopted enthusiastically in both the United States and Canada. In domestic architecture, there was little regional variation in the basic plan, which was usually chosen from a pattern book, but ornamentation reached new heights in the hands of builders and carpenters. Materials included wood and shingles, brick or stone, terra-cotta panels and turned posts for porches and balustrades. Stained glass was often used for hall and staircase windows, and bay windows might include small tinted panes outlining the top sash. Towers of every form—round, square and octagonal—sprouted from various parts of the house, which was often painted in five or six colors to emphasize the detailing. Virtually every surface was textured or appliquéd to add visual interest.

Below: *Burgeoning San Francisco showed off its affluence in exuberant townhouses like this one, with its multiple window treatments, decorative tower and pediment, and imaginative scrollwork, fanlights and pilasters.*

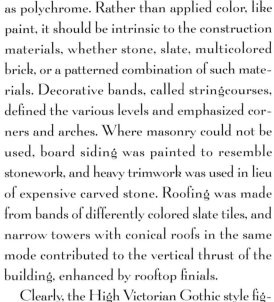

Interiors gained new flexibility, with large, open ground-floor plans designed around a central stair hall. Sliding doors were used to separate the common rooms or to join them when a larger space was needed, as for entertaining. Many windows contributed to ample ventilation and natural lighting. Some of the pattern books included plans for interior design, landscaping, even furniture style, and interior features included rich woodwork and plasterwork, built-in bookcases and cabinets and glazed tile fireplace surrounds. Balance was achieved by alternating vertical and horizontal elements, plain surfaces and decorative elements.

The Romanesque Revival in the United States was dominated by several gifted architects, one of whom was James Renwick, who designed the original Smithsonian Institution building, known as "the Castle," in 1846. More frequently seen in public buildings than in domestic architecture, it was characterized by square towers, hipped roofs and gables and decorative detailing of medieval inspiration. Its most influential exponent was Henry Hobson Richardson, who created an indigenous style exemplified by Boston's Trinity Church (1872). Its features included rough-faced (rusticated) masonry walls, massive arched entrances with short columns, deeply set windows, heavy stone stringcourses and asymmetrically placed circular towers with conical roofs. Richardson's influence was so predominant that this later style is usually identified as Richardsonian Romanesque. He designed only a few houses, but his work inspired other architects all over the country during the late nineteenth century. Perhaps his best-known house is the one designed for John Glessner in Chicago in 1885. In its less expensive variation, the Shingle style, Richardson created a distinctive American resort house, of which most examples occur on the East Coast.

Usually considered Victorian, but, in fact, post-Victorian in chronology, are the distinctive Norman, Chateauesque and Tudor Revival styles of the turn of the century. As their names suggest, the first two borrowed heavily from the medieval architecture of northern France and

the Loire Valley. The Chateauesque style originated in France as the revival of a sixteenth-century style (often known as François I) that was popularized by the influential *École des Beaux Arts*. The best-known American example is the Biltmore estate, designed for George W. Vanderbilt by Richard Morris Hunt in 1895 as a North Carolina summer home. The expense of the Chateauesque style precluded its use for most domestic architecture.

The Tudor Revival style was more readily adapted to vernacular architecture, and examples are still seen across the nation. Eclectic in inspiration, the Tudor house drew freely upon late-medieval English prototypes. Its stylistic features include steeply pitched gabled roofs, façades dominated by a prominent cross gable with decorative half-timbering, tall narrow windows, stucco cladding and large chimneys. The popularity of this style was rivaled only by the contemporaneous Georgian or "Colonial Revival" discussed in the previous chapter.

Above: *The best-known Victorian mansion in the United States is the William McKendric Carson house in Eureka, California (1885). More than 100 carpenters worked in every kind of wood on the world market to create the hand-carved Eastlake ornamentation of this eighteen-room house. The Second-Empire style main house, elaborate finials, roof cresting, stickwork and carved moldings are among its most striking features.*

Stick-style Houses

Ornamental stickwork on building exteriors became fashionable in the East about 1865 as a development of the Cottage style popularized by A.J. Downing. The example at right, in Clinton, New Jersey, alternates vertical and horizontal members on the two front-facing gables. A more elaborate incarnation is the Downs-Aldrich House below, built in 1893 in Crockett, Texas. On the opposite page is a beautiful Bayview, Michigan, home with typical Stick-style asymmetrical massing and broad-roofed porches with turned posts, decorative brackets and geometric balustrades.

Townhouses and Suburban Villas

The Montreal townhouses above have elaborate mansard rooflines with hooded windows of generous size to illuminate the top floor. Masonry construction was the norm in French Canada from the seventeenth century. On the opposite page is a delightful Rockport, Maine, house that combines French Empire and Italianate features. At left, a faithfully restored "painted lady" on the Connecticut coast, near Mystic. Note the harmonious gable, balcony and porch ornamentation.

Picturesque Queen Anne Country Houses

Above is a classic refined Queen Anne home in Woodstock, New Brunswick, beautifully located and commanding a hilltop view. On the opposite page (top) is Wilderstein, a Queen Anne-style mansion in Rhinebeck, New York, that evolved from an 1852 Italianate villa with the help of architect Arnout Cannon, Jr. He added the five-story tower, third floor, verandahs and other features in the late 1880s. The spacious and welcoming house opposite, below, with its wraparound porch and conical tower roofs, was built in Westport, Connecticut, in 1899.

Queen Anne: Apogee of the Victorian Styles

Projecting pavilions, porches and decorative towers are the focal points of these Victorian mansions of the late nineteenth century. The house above is a Texas-size Queen Anne—the W.B. Houston House, built in 1895 in Gonzales, with arched openings that contrast with the vertical thrust of the towers, finials and columns.

At top right is the impressive Ann Starrett Mansion (1889) in Port Wilson, Washington, then a booming lumber town. The impeccably restored painted lady at right is an Indiana Historic Landmark with a beveled tower, massive brick chimneys, generous porch and small pediments above the entry and at second-story level.

Romanesque and Chateauesque Mansions

These late-century styles were often combined, as in these masonry mansions that feature both the rough-cut stone facing and prominent arches of the Richardsonian Romanesque and the fanciful towers of the medieval Loire Valley.

Above and opposite, top, are two Detroit, Michigan, landmarks—Whitney House, and the imposing F.J. Hecker House; at right, The Bishop's Palace Mansion by Nicholas Clayton (1886) in Galveston, Texas.

The Norman Style

The Tyler, Texas, mansion above and the fieldstone Montreal townhouse at left illustrate that Norman-style buildings featured bolder, more massive forms and minimal ornamentation vis-á-vis the Queen Anne, High Victorian Gothic and other elaborate houses of the eclectic nineteenth century.

The country houses of France's Normandy region had an influence on American and Canadian architecture from about 1885, primarily in the East. Opposite, top is a handsome Toronto, Canada, structure with Renaissance detailing and the hipped roof, tall chimney and rounded turret characteristic of the Norman style.

Victoriana in British Columbia

The scenic beauties of British Columbia made Vancouver Island a mecca for artists and travelers once Canada's transcontinental railroad was completed. At right is Burrville, a high-style Queen Anne heritage house in Deas Island Regional Park. The impeccable Victorian below was the home of painter Emily Carr, a native of Victoria, who immortalized the region's landscapes and native peoples in her work. On the opposite page is the delightful rambling resort called The Aerie, commanding a breathtaking view of Vancouver Island's natural wonders.

San Francisco's Painted Ladies (overleaf)

These historic Victorian townhouses on Alamo Square have been faithfully restored to their original beauty and present a dazzling array of surface textures, ornamental pediments, bay windows, arched entryways, cornices and balustrades in Queen Anne-style profusion. San Francisco preservationists were instrumental in showing how a city's architectural treasures could be renewed, rather than razed in misguided attempts to modernize.

Details and Decorations

Ornamental features of every kind offer valuable clues to the period and style of North American houses. Window treatments, or fenestration, for example, are among the most telling details. The word window comes from "wind hole"—the original function of small openings in the sides of a shelter, which was to ventilate and admit light. Such openings had to be covered with hide or oiled paper when the weather was cold or wet, as seen in the oldest colonial buildings on the continent.

Once glass became more widely available, the humble wind hole assumed an increasing variety of forms. More substantial colonial houses in the Georgian style usually had double-hung sash windows with six to nine panes in each sash and a semicircular Palladian window above. Most French colonial houses of the Mississippi Valley region had casement windows flanked by vertical-board shutters with horizontal battens that could be closed at night and in bad weather. Classical Revival houses often had circular or fan-shaped windows in pedimented gables, or small pediments above sash windows arranged in symmetrical patterns. The Victorian era saw a host of styles, including Italianate windows with curved tops and U-shaped hoods or moldings, and picturesque oval and octagonal windows in the gable of Gothic Revival cottages ornamented with "gingerbread" woodwork. The various Cottage styles harked back to European prototypes and often featured casement windows opening onto flowering window boxes. Most had larger panes than those of true

medieval form — with small diamond-shaped glazing. Queen Anne Revival houses often show small colored panes inset around a clear-glass center and groups of three or four windows on projecting bays or towers.

In many instances, doorways were treated much like the other façade openings—the windows—with numerous variations from one

Opposite: *A multitextured Queen Anne Revival façade in historic Cape May, New Jersey.*

Below: *A beautiful leaded-glass window at Michigan's E.E. Ford mansion.*

Above: *A classical broken pediment with sunburst motifs and centered finial.*

Right: *A fluted column on a Southport, Connecticut, house with an ornate capital of botanical inspiration.*

style to another. Greek Revival houses often had full-height porticoes with symmetrical doors and windows behind them, crowned by individual pediments. The Georgian style shows restrained ornamentation in the form of pilasters and rectangular sidelights flanking the entrance, with a modest pediment above. Romanesque houses have wide archways of stone or brick, with the doors deeply recessed in an entry porch. The log cabin generally had a sturdy plank door with a deerskin

latchstring that closed it tightly at night but was "let out" by day to admit light, air and visitors—always welcome on the isolated frontier. The baled-hay and sod houses of the Great Plains had timber-framed doorways that helped to support the structure. Working-class rowhouses usually had identical doors facing a narrow stoop on which families and neighbors could escape hot summer nights in the city and congregate during the day to watch the children play stickball, "kick the can" and other outdoor games.

Color, too, has much to tell us about regional styles, climate and materials. As Lewis Mumford observed in *Sticks and Stones* (Dover, 1924): "The aesthetic reason for delighting in white colonial farmhouses is simple; white and white alone fully reflects the surrounding light...[and] gives a pure blue or lavender shadow against the sunlight." Southern plantation houses, too, were commonly painted white to reflect the sun and cool the interiors. In the heyday of the Greek Revival, all kinds of buildings were reclad or repainted to simulate the appearance of marble.

Natural materials including wood, shingling, brick, fieldstone and cut stone usually weather to muted colors that harmonize with the natural setting and create a sense of strength and durability. Appliqué materials like terra-cotta panels and tiling are more susceptible to wear, but add distinction to multitextured surfaces like those of the Queen Anne and Exotic Revivals. Exterior paint, of course, also requires constant upkeep, and the delightful color harmonies of recently restored Victorian houses show how painting can be used as an art form on residential architecture. San Francisco colorist Bob Buckter has done some 400 color designs for California's Bay Area houses alone, and many other designers and craftspeople are reviving skills that were rapidly disappearing in the postmodern era.

Decorative metalwork was a feature of colonial architecture in the form of weathervanes, wrought-iron hinges and other handmade ornaments. It became increasingly popular during the nineteenth century, when iron foundries and factories produced ornamental cresting for rooflines, decorative hinges and other hardware, curving handrails for stairways, lacy balustrades and fencing for city houses on narrow lots. Metal roofing came into use, especially on vernacular houses in the South and West, where it helped reflect the sun's glare and cool the interior.

The Victorian Carpenter Gothic, Stick and Eastlake styles allowed woodworkers to reach new heights of fantasy in producing applied trim in the form of fretwork, sunbursts, finials, diagonal and ripple-effect stickwork, curved shingles, spoolwork and gable ornaments. Popular pattern books and builders' manuals circulated widely, and by the late nineteenth century certain motifs could be found from coast to coast.

The British Garden Suburb movement, and the aesthetic of the picturesque, created growing interest in landscaping and garden ornaments that completed the ideal home. As described by author Tony Hiss in *The Experience of Place*, this optimum environment is one that nurtures a variety of human needs "so pervasive and so fundamental that...we have to have places around us that nourish our eyes, our ears and all our senses simultaneously to be able to flourish as human beings and feel at home with ourselves." John Ruskin would have applauded this sentiment, as would Davis and Downing.

Architectural fashions, like the fashions we wear, tend to come back into vogue again and again, using new materials to recreate enduring designs. This has been the case with the long-lived Georgian style, most recently reprised as "Colonial architecture" in the United States, along with the New England garrison house and the durable Cape Cod. Similarly, the delicate classical detailing popularized by the Adam brothers in eighteenth-century England was transplanted to the United States in the post-revolutionary Federal style, and its ornate garlands, swags and urns reappeared as design elements in the late Victorian era.

The first true American architects left an indelible imprint on the ornaments of our major cities, including Charles Bulfinch (Boston),

William Jay (Savannah, Georgia), Benjamin H. Latrobe (Philadelphia and Virginia) and Samuel McIntire (Salem, Massachusetts). Initially, both French Canada and the original thirteen British colonies looked to the mother countries for inspiration, but as national confidence and prosperity increased, a new generation of native-born architects adapted, embellished and created indigenous forms from Quebec City to Vancouver Island, New York City to San Francisco. The images that follow provide a glimpse of the decorative details that have added so much to the rich vocabulary of North American architecture, from its tentative beginnings to its present stature as a leader in the art of residential design.

Below: *Steeply gabled slate roofs and medieval-style chimney pots at the Edsel E. Ford mansion, Michigan.*

Colonial Doorways

On the opposite page, a bold pedimented doorway in the Deerfield, Massachusetts, style, flanked by fluted pilasters. This Pioneer Valley home in Old Deerfield dates from the early 1700s, as seen in the diagonal and cross bracing on the doors and the small-paned transoms above them. At right is an elegant Adam-style house in Newport, Rhode Island. The delicate doorway fanlight with keystone above is reprised in the pedimented gable. Paired stairways with an iron balustrade complete this classical entryway. The colonial house below, in Thompson Hill, Connecticut, has a decorative appleboard above the front door: the pineapple motif is a traditional sign of welcome.

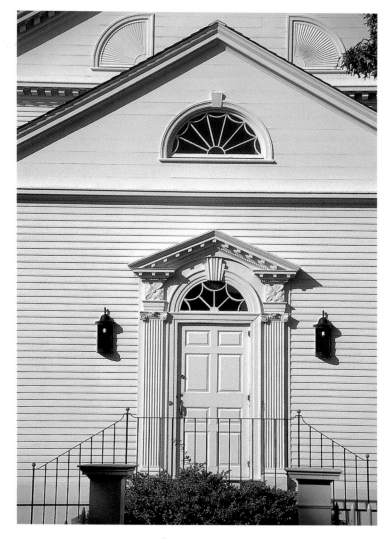

Symmetrical Window Treatments

Small-paned casement and dormer windows in white surrounds line the fieldstone walls of Montreal's Chateau Ramezay, opposite, above, built in French Canada in 1705. The traditional Quebec townhouse took on its present form in the early eighteenth century, with detailing inspired by the classicism fashionable in the mother country. Later examples are seen in New York City's Gramercy Park (above and opposite, below). The brownstone façade above has floor-length French windows crowned by simple pediments at street level and narrow sash windows above. The brick house opposite, below, has deeply recessed French windows in ornamental curved surrounds painted white to contrast with the brick. Low wrought-iron balustrades draped in climbing plants overlook the green oasis of fenced Gramercy Park, to which residents of the square hold keys.

Decorative Nineteenth-century Entryways

On the opposite page, an elliptical fanlight with wrought-iron design work surmounts an impressive paneled Dutch-style door and fanlights framed by fluted pilasters on this Thomaston, Maine, residence. The architectural treasures of New York's Hudson Valley include Wyndcliffe (below), at Rhinebeck, a Norman-style mansion with geometric brickwork framing the entrance. At right, is a detail from Olana, the Moorish villa designed by Calvert Vaux for artist Frederic Edwin Church, complete with Middle Eastern arches and geometric tile inlays.

Ornamental Gables

The Victorian era rose to new heights of ornament, as seen on the opposite page in the Stick-style gable (above) and the richly textured Queen Anne example (below). At right and below are exuberant Carpenter Gothic gable ornaments, including bold finials, scrollwork, pointed arches and the oculus windows below, inset with a quatrefoil design.

Romanesque Towers

Sturdy round towers with conical roofs were popular with late-nineteenth-century designers. The example at right is decorated in the eclectic Queen Anne style, while the shorter masonry tower below, with arched openings framed by rugged stonework, is in the manner of Henry Hobson Richardson.

Polygonal Towers and Roof Projections

The bracketed Italianate style often took the form of two-story towers like the one at right, with round-arched, paired windows at the second level, overhung by wide eaves. The wall surfaces are defined by moldings. The Belfast, Maine, Victorian house below has a picturesque roof projection with flared eaves, a pointed window and a carved gable decoration in the Eastlake style.

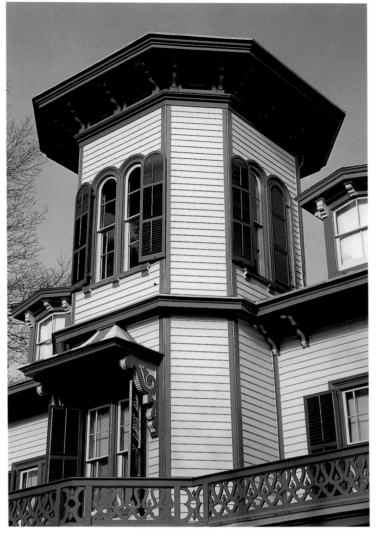

Queen Anne Appliqué and Texturing

The diversity of Queen Anne-style ornamentation is seen in these examples, which combine an incredible array of Victorian details. The paired dormer window surround above has painted and appliquéd decoration, including a bowed cornice and brackets contrasted against fish-scale shingling. At left, a detail profusely ornamented with leaf and flower motifs, highlighted by arches and dentils. The arched entryways on the opposite page combine spoolwork and ornaments (above) and botanically inspired appliqué of the type that characterized the earlier Adam style. Exquisite coloring adds greatly to the overall effect.

Scrollwork, Sunbursts and Cutouts

Ornamental cast-iron fencing (left) added the finishing touch to many nineteenth-century stairways, balconies and front yards, especially in the South. Flat cut-out balustrades like the ones below, and opposite, below, were favored for informal chalet-style houses of Swiss and German inspiration. Stylized sunbursts like the gable ornaments on the opposite page, top, were popular in both the United States and Canada during the late Victorian era.

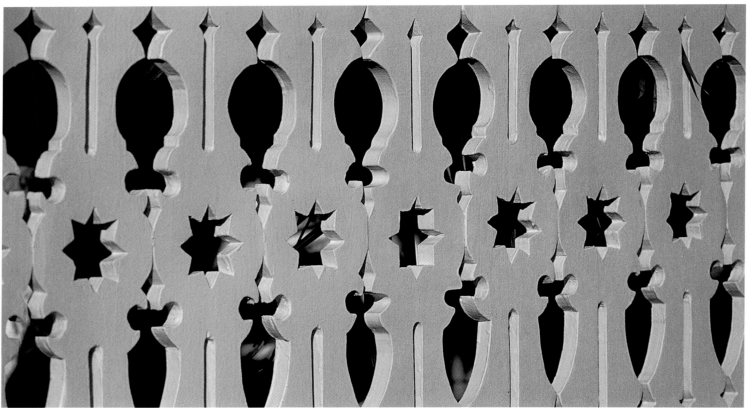

Gardens and Gateways (overleaf)

A montage of outdoor scenes reflecting the deep affinity between our natural and manmade landscapes across the continent.

Glossary of Architectural Terms

acroterion A pedestal for a sculpture or ornament at the base or apex of a pediment.

architrave The lowermost part of an entablature, resting directly on top of a column in classical architecture.

ashlar The square-edged hewn stones for wall construction laid in horizontal courses with vertical joints.

balustrade A row of miniature columns (balusters) supporting a handrail, used decoratively to frame porches and crown rooftops.

batten A narrow strip of wood used for flooring and siding in alternation with wider boards (called board-and-batten).

bargeboard The projecting boards placed against the gable ends of buildings and usually decorated, as in the Victorian mode.

belt course A change of exterior masonry or patterning used to articulate the stories of a building; also called stringcourse.

buttress A masonry pier used to reinforce exterior walls.

cantilever A projecting beam or other structure supported at only one end.

capital The top part of a column, usually decorated, and larger than the column shaft.

casement window A narrow window with sashes that open outward on hinges.

cladding A finishing material, like boards or shingles, overlaid on an unfinished wall or roof, whether of timber framing, masonry, or other material.

clapboard A thin board laid horizontally and overlapped to create a weathertight surface on a wooden building.

colonnade A row of columns, often with horizontal entablature.

corbel A masonry block projecting from a wall to support a horizontal feature.

cornice A projecting, usually decorative, feature at the top of walls, arches and eaves.

crenelation A pattern of square indentations of medieval inspiration, also called battlements.

dentil One of a series of small rectangular blocks forming a decorative molding, or projecting beneath a cornice.

dogtrot A roofed passage or breezeway between two parts of a vernacular house, especially a log cabin.

dormer A vertically positioned window set into a sloping roof.

eaves The lower edge of a roof that projects beyond the wall below.

entablature The upper section of a classical order, resting on the capital and including the architrave, frieze and cornice.

Fachwerk A German method of timber construction.

fanlight A semicircular window, often with sash bars arranged like the ribs of a fan.

fenestration The arrangement of the windows in a building.

finial A vertical ornament fixed to the peak of a roof or tower, used especially in Gothic styles.

fretwork An ornamental feature consisting of three-dimensional geometric designs or other symmetrical figures (frets) enclosed in a band or border.

friezeboard A decorative band around a wall.

gable A triangular wall area enclosed by the rising edges of a sloping roof.

gambrel roof A ridged roof with two slopes on each side, the lower slope having the steeper pitch. Often used on barns and neo-Dutch colonial buildings.

half-timbering A type of timber-frame construction in which the surfaces between posts and beams are filled in with another material, like stucco or brick, leaving part of the timber framing exposed.

hip roof One with sloping ends and sides, on which each external angle is formed by the meeting of two adjacent sloping sides.

jetty A second story projecting over the first-story façade.

joists The parallel beams that support a floor or ceiling.

lintel A horizontal beam or stone placed over door or window openings.

loggia A gallery or arcade open to the air on one or both sides.

mansard roof One with a double slope on all four sides, the lower slope being steeper than the upper.

modillion A small bracket supporting a cornice.

mullion A slender vertical bar used in dividing the panes of a window.

oculus window A circular window in the upper story or the dome of a building.

ogee arch An arch of two curves meeting at a point, as in Oriental architecture; also, a double curve with the shape of an elongated "S."

oriel window The upper-story bay window supported by a corbel or bracket.

parapet A low wall or railing along the edge of a roof or balcony.

pediment A low triangular element, framed by horizontal sloping cornices, usually found at the gable ends of a Greek temple between the frieze and the roof; most often used in residential architecture as a decorative element over doorways.

pent roof A narrow single-sloped roof often used to protect entrances.

pier A supporting post, usually square, shorter and thicker than a column.

pilaster A shallow pier attached to a wall, usually rectangular, used especially for decoration of doorways and fireplaces.

portico A colonnaded entry porch.

post-and-girt construction The timber framing joined by hand-hewn notches.

quatrefoil An ornament composed of four clover-like lobes radiating from a common center and offset by triangular cusps between each lobe.

quoin A rectangle of stone or brick used in a vertical series to decorate the corners of a building and façade openings.

sash The framework or mullion that holds the glass in a window.

sidelights The long, narrow windows flanking a doorway.

siding The boards, shingles, or other material used to surface a frame building.

sill plate The horizontal timber at base level that supports the uprights of a building frame.

stepped gable One constructed with a series of steps or curves along the roof slope, but independent of it. Often seen in Flemish and German architecture.

stickwork The exterior patterned woodwork that serves an ornamental rather than a structural purpose.

stringcourse see **beltcourse**

stucco A durable finish for exterior walls, usually composed of cement, sand and lime.

stud One of a series of vertical wood or metal structural members in a wall frame.

transom A narrow horizontal window, usually placed over a door to admit additional light.

tab A wedge-shaped stone or brick used to form ornamental patterns in masonry façades (French, *voussoir*).

vault An arched roof or ceiling, as in a rotunda.

vigas The rough-hewn timber roof supports projecting from the upper façade of Pueblo-style and Hispanic buildings.

Bibliography

Byers, Mary, and Margaret McBurney. *Atlantic Hearth: Early Homes and Families of Nova Scotia*. Toronto: Univ. of Toronto Press, 1994.

Clark, Clifford Edward, Jr. *The American Family Home: 1800–1960*. Chapel Hill: Univ. of North Carolina Press, 1986.

Dixon, Roger, and Stefan Muthesius. *Victorian Architecture*, World of Art series. London: Thames and Hudson, 1978.

Guild, Robin. *The Victorian House Book*. N.Y.: Rizzoli, 1989.

Kemp, Jim. *American Vernacular: Regional Influences in Architecture and Interior Design*. N.Y.: Viking Penguin, 1987.

Maitland, Leslie, et al. *A Guide to Canadian Architectural Styles*. Peterborough, Ont.: Broadview Press, 1992.

Pomada, Elizabeth, and Michael Larsen. *America's Painted Ladies: The Ultimate Celebration of Our Victorians*. N.Y.: Penguin Books USA/Viking Studio Books, 1992.

Poppliers, John C., et al. *What Style Is It? A Guide to American Architecture*, Building Watchers series. Wash., D.C.: National Trust for Historic Preservation, 1983.

Risotti, Howard, and Kenneth K. Trapp. *Skilled Work: American Craft in the Renwick Gallery*. Wash., D.C.: Smithsonian Institution Press, 1998.

Sommer, Robin Langley, with Balthazar Korab. *American Architecture: Colonial Styles to the Present Day*. Rowayton, Conn.: Saraband, 1998.

Upton, Dell, ed. *America's Architectural Roots: Ethnic Groups That Built America*, Building Watchers series. Wash., D.C.: National Trust for Historic Preservation, 1986.

Walker, Lester. *American Shelter: An Illustrated Encyclopedia of the American House*. Woodstock, N.Y.: Overlook Press, 1981.

Acknowledgements

The publisher would like to thank the following individuals for their assistance in the preparation of this book: Sara Hunt and Nicola J. Gillies, editors; Charles J. Ziga, art director and photographer; Wendy Ciaccia Eurell, graphic designer; Lisa Langone Desautels, indexer; Jay Olstad for supplementary research and photography; and Annie Lise Roberts for her architecture expertise. Grateful acknowledgement is also made to the owners of the featured homes, travel and tourism agencies, historical societies across the continent and the photographers and agencies listed below for permission to reproduce the photographs on the following pages: © Kindra Clineff 1999 : 7, 82, 126, 127b; © Rudi Holnsteiner: 19, 26–27, 45, 46, 47, 48–49tr, 50b, 50–51t, 53t, 54b, 56–57, 58, 60, 64b, 66, 67, 68t, 68–69b, 70–71, 72, 73b, 86, 87, 88, 89, 96, 97b, 101, 107b, 112–13t, 115b, 116–17t; © Balthazar Korab: 12, 14, 16, 23b, 42, 44, 48tl &b, 54t, 55, 59, 65b, 69tr, 74b, 75, 76, 77t, 78, 81, 83, 85t, 90, 98, 106, 114, 115t, 123, 125, 127t, 141t; © Jay Olstad: 9b, 39t, 69tl, 74t, 77b, 79, 85b, 111t, 131, 134t; © 1999 Michael A. Smith: 4r, 52t; © John Sylvester: 17, 34, 35, 93b, 94b, 100, 110; © Charles J. Ziga: 1, 2, 4 (l & c), 5, 6, 8–9, 10, 11, 13, 15, 18, 20, 21, 22, 24, 25, 28, 29, 31, 32, 33, 36, 37, 38, 39b, 40, 41, 51b, 52–53b, 84, 91, 92, 94t, 95, 97t, 99, 102, 103, 104, 105, 107t, 108, 109, 111b, 113t, 116t & b, 120–21, 122, 124, 128, 129, 130, 132, 133, 134b, 135, 136, 137, 138, 139, 141b; Canadian Tourism Commission Photo: 63 (Yves Beaulieu); Corbis: 118 (© Gunter Marx), 119t (© Wolfgang Kaehler), 119b (© Gunter Marx); FPG International LLC: 30 (© Peter Gridley 1994); Historical Landmarks Foundation of Indiana: 80, 113b; Prints and Photographs Division, Library of Congress: 62; Santa Fe CVB: 64–65t (© Chris Corrie), 140 (© Chris Corrie); Southern Indiana Clark & Floyd Counties: 23t; Vermont Department of Tourism & Marketing: 93t; Wisconsin Department of Tourism: 73t (© Robert Granflaten).

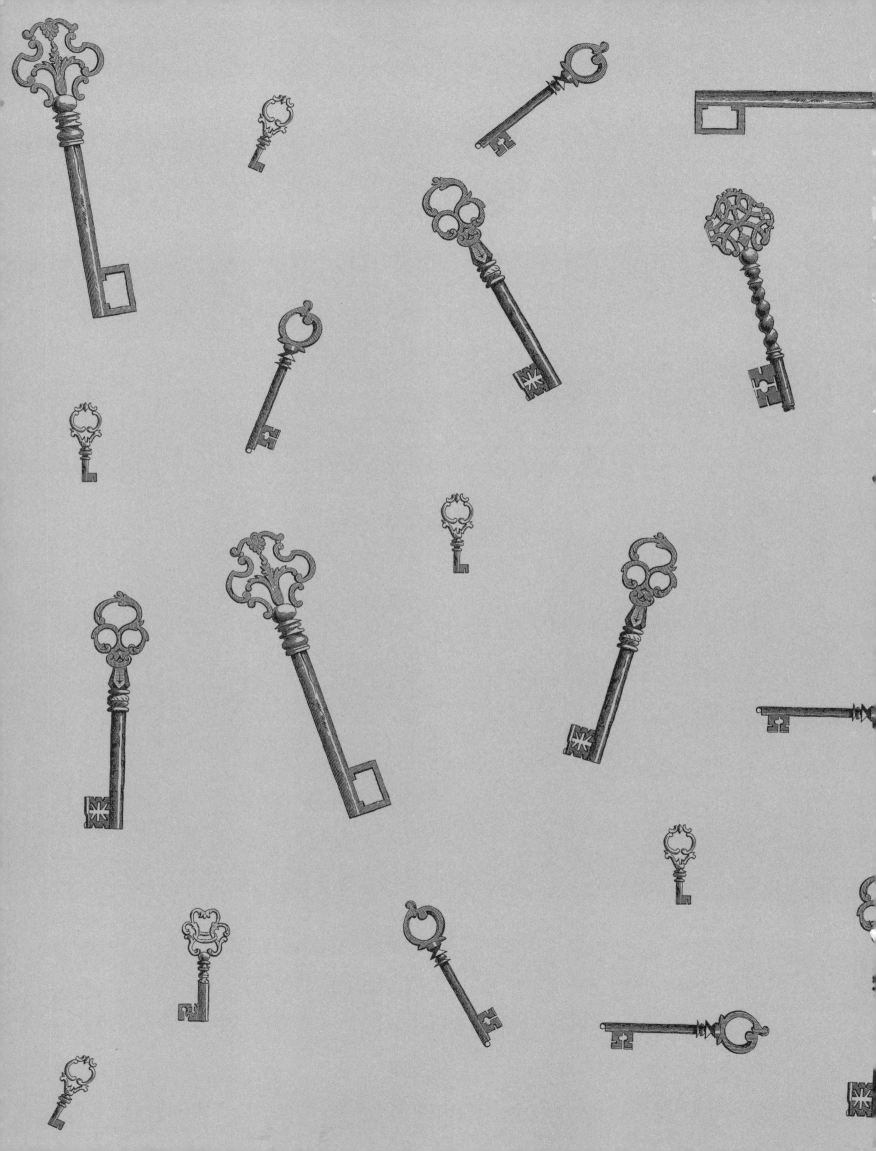